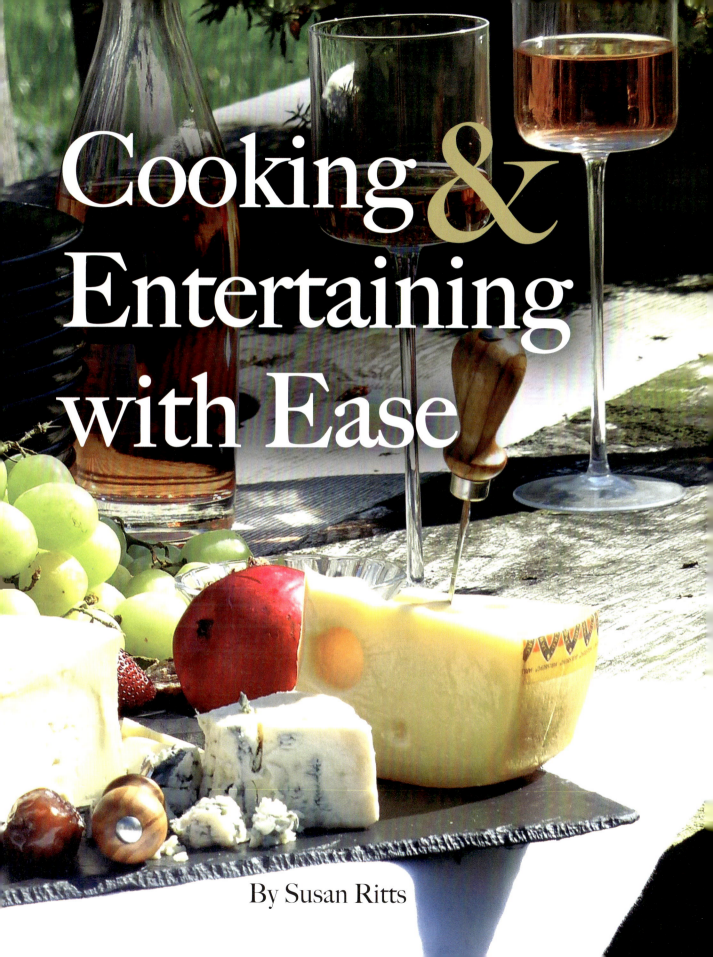

Cooking & Entertaining with Ease

Susan Ritts

Photographs by:
Laura Von Hagen

Contributing Photographers:
Amy Dickson, Dan Dondanville and
Susan Ritts

RITTS
publishing

Copyright © 2016 by Susan Ritts

Photographs copyright © 2016 by Laura Von Hagen, Susan Ritts, Dan Dondandville, and Amy Dickson

All rights reserved in accordance with the U.S. Copyright Act of 1976, the scanning, uploading, and electronic sharing of any part of this book without the permission of the publisher constitute unlawful piracy and theft of the author's intellectual property. If you would like to use material from the book (other than for review purposes), prior written permission must be obtained by contacting the publisher.

Published by Ritts Publishing
Maple Plain, Minnesota
www.rittspublishing.com

Printed in the United States of America

First Edition: November 2016
10 9 8 7 6 5 4 3 2 1

Library of Congress Cataloging-in Publication Data is available upon request. ISBN 978-0-9981617-0-9

Thank you for adding *Cooking & Entertaining with Ease* to your cookbook collection

Over the years I have had the good fortune to explore my passion for food through work, play and travel. This book reflects years of culinary experimenting and tasting, note-taking and research.

In this cookbook, you will find some uncomplicated, delicious recipes that are not just mine, but also some of my favorites from friends and family. I've included photos of my outdoor flower gardens which have evolved into entertaining "rooms." My husband Chris, and I have also woven in beautiful vegetable gardens that provide much of the fresh produce for my recipes. As we not only love to cook, but truly enjoy entertaining, I've shared party ideas, some of which have become annual events we simply tweak each year.

So settle back with a good bottle of wine and peruse the recipes, gardens and parties. Then plan your first meal – or party…..or both!

-Susan Ritts

To Chris and Molly. Your encouragement and support has been invaluable. Love you both.

Contents

Introduction - 5

Recommended Pantry Items - 8

Parties & Events - 10

Appetizers - 24

Chilis, Soups, Salads & Stews - 60

Meat, Potatoes & Mexican Dishes - 90

Pasta & Rice - 120

Sandwiches - 138

Sweets - 152

About the Author - 172

Acknowledgments - 173

YOUR PANTRY:
ITEMS TO HAVE ON HAND

Try to keep the following in your pantry as these can be used weekly, if not daily:

HIGH QUALITY OLIVE OIL	REAL BUTTER
FLOUR	CAKE FLOUR
SUGAR	BAKING SODA & POWDER
WHITE VINEGAR	SALAD VINEGAR
VEGETABLE OIL	WORCESTERSHIRE SAUCE
KETCHUP	DIJON MUSTARD
SHORTENING	CORN STARCH
ASSORTED SPICES *(including salt & pepper)*	

COMMON COOKING TERMS

ROUX (PRONOUNCED ROO)
A roux is a flour paste used to thicken soups and sauces. A roux is 2 parts flour to 1 part butter. To make a roux, melt 2 tablespoons butter in a sauce pan. Add 4 tablespoons flour to the butter and cook, stirring until a paste forms and the color is a light sandy color or light brown. Add to your hot soup or sauce, stirring until combined. Soup/sauce should thicken. If more is needed, or your soup/sauce is quite large, increase the size of the roux.

SEAR
To sear meat is to briefly cook meat on all sides in a large, very hot frying pan to form a crust. Each side is seared about 3 minutes to obtain the crust.

BRAISE
To braise meat is to first sear meat on each side and then cook meat in a pot at a lower temperature with liquids. The pulled pork recipe in this book is an example of braising the meat after its been seared.

CLARIFIED BUTTER
Clarified butter is unsalted butter that is heated/melted to separate the liquids and the milk solids, which float to the top and are skimmed off, leaving clarified butter. Clarified butter has a higher smoke point, making it preferable to cook with for some recipes.

MINCE
To mince ingredients simply means to chop very finely.

BRINE
A combination of salt and water in which meat is soaked to tenderize and plump. Usually 4 tablespoons salt to 4 cups water. It can have other spices in it as well. Large pieces of meat, such as a whole chicken, should be brined 8-12 hours. Smaller pieces, 1-4 hours.

Parties & Events

Outdoor Summer Party

Football Tailgate
Hot Weather Game
Cold Weather Game

Fall Barn Party

Girls Ornament Exchange

Holiday Bus Party

OUTDOOR SUMMER PARTY

Chris and I throw an annual summer party at our farm and invite every fun person we know – and we know a lot of fun people. My friend Charlie is in a band and they play every year – I took up drumming a few years back so they have to let me play a few songs with them!

To make sure no one drives after a few cold beers, car keys are confiscated and guests plan to stay and pitch tents all over the property. Several meals are served – BBQ dinner, late night sandwiches and Sunday brunch. Our menus are below. Super fun. Great food and music too!

DINNER MENU

Pulled pork sandwiches *(page 104)*
Wisconsin bratwurst
Red cabbage coleslaw *(page 86)*
Watermelon wedges
Ice cream bars

Extra long hot dogs
Traditional potato salad *(page 115)*
Grilled corn on the cob with melted butter "bath"

Condiments to accompany pulled pork and dogs/brats: Ketchup, BBQ sauce, spicy mustard, chopped onion, relish, shredded Cheddar cheese, sliced jalapeños and pepperoncini peppers.

We light Chinese lanterns around the property before the band starts and enjoy their floating beauty all evening. Around 11 p.m. it's snack time! So I pull out round two of food – French sandwiches. The next morning we serve brunch.

BRUNCH MENU
DRINKS

Have 2 small plates on the bar. Put water on one plate and sea salt on the other. Prior to making Bloodies, guests can dip their glasses in the water and then in the salt for salt-rimmed cocktail glasses.

Orange juice
Spicy tomato juice
Vodka
Celery, dill pickles and olives

Mimosas & Bloody Marys
Champagne
Salt

FOOD

Mom's ham strata casserole *(page 108)*
Bacon & sausage
Bagels with plain and jalapeño cream cheese

Scrambled eggs with cheese
Hash brown potatoes
Toast

Set up a buffet area for all food and a bar area for drinks. To make it a bit easier for you, have a toaster plugged in on or near the buffet table accompanied by bread/bagels, cream cheese and butter. An awesome way to end a memorable weekend!

FOOTBALL TAILGATE

My family has a long history at Notre Dame University and sister school Saint Mary's College in South Bend, Indiana. As huge football fans, we love to host tailgate parties for my daughter Molly and many nieces, nephews and friends who are carrying on the Notre Dame tradition.

As football season starts as early as the end of August, the climate needs to be taken into consideration. It's usually still quite hot at the first couple of games, so I always make sure foods provided can withstand the temperature. Any food that needs to be kept cold sits in an ice bath — plus we always set up an overhead tent to protect both food and people from heat or rain.

Make sure you have one or two collapsible tables, tablecloths and flowers. You will also need 3 or 4 coolers and LOTS of ice. My sister Anne brings a cool Notre Dame centerpiece as well—always a fun surprise!

HOT WEATHER GAME MENU
DRINKS

Several coolers of iced beer (restock as needed)
Vodka
Tomato juice
A variety of different flavor soft drinks
Drink Condiments: Olives, dill pickles, celery and seasoned Salt

Several bottles of champagne
Orange juice
Bottled water

HOT WEATHER GAME MENU
FOOD

Hosting tip: Cook sandwiches prior to leaving for the game. They will stay warm in wrapped foil and are excellent at room temperature as well.

Flank Steak Sandwiches (page 143)
Ham & Cheese French Sandwiches (page 142)
Potato Skins with sour cream (page 31)
Egg Salad Dip with crackers (page 38)
Chocolate Chip Cookies with Sea Salt (page 156)
Blue and gold cupcakes (or your team's colors)
Bowls of assorted nuts
Food condiments: Horseradish sauce, mustard, salt & pepper

Buffalo Mozzarella, Avocado & Tomato Sandwiches (page 149)
Large grilled shrimp with cocktail sauce (page 32)
Bowls of assorted nuts
Watermelon wedges

Cooking & Entertaining with Ease

FOOTBALL TAILGATE: COLD WEATHER MENU

Bring double the amount of Sterno needed under pans to replace each if needed.

COLD WEATHER GAME MENU
FOOD

Meatballs *(page 126)*
Pigs in a blanket
Chili with topping *(page 74)*
Bowls of nuts

BBQ Chicken Drummies *(page 106)*
Potato Skins *(page 31)*
Veggie tray
Chocolate Chip Cookies with Sea Salt *(page 156)*

Condiments: Spicy mustard, ketchup, sour cream, BBQ sauce

Hosting tip: Set up separate pans of chicken & ribs, pigs in a blanket, potato skins and meatballs. Put two cans of Sterno beneath each pan. Bring chili in a large fondue pot or other large pot with a stand that Sterno may be placed under. Bring extra cans of Sterno so you can replace as needed. Relax, get your game-face on, have a beer and enjoy!

FALL BARN PARTY

Chris and I have an old dairy barn on our property, and as we have no cows, we converted part of the barn into an entertaining room. This area has a built-in stage (where the hay was kept), so it is perfect for our band parties. We throw some rugs down, set up chairs and benches, stock up the wine barrel bar and voila! Barn party is ready to go. Food is set up buffet-style in the house so guests wander back and forth enjoying food, music and each other.

DINNER MENU

DRINKS
Beer   **Sangria**
Pop   **Water**

APPETIZERS
Guacamole, salsa & homemade tortilla chips *(page 36 & 37)*
Egg Salad Spread/Dip & crackers *(page 38)*
Apple Cheese Crustini *(page 52)*

FOOD
Flank Steak Sandwiches *(page 143)*
Arugula & Spinach Salad *(page 76)*
Green Onion & Olive Oil Potato Salad *(page 116)*
Watermelon Slices
Chocolate Chip Cookies with Sea Salt *(page 156)*
Lemon Bars *(page 166)*

Later in the evening the band has packed up but iTunes favorites are playing. The party is still going full steam and dancing is burning calories. As always the second round of food emerges to satisfy late-night snackers. A variety of the French sandwiches is served—Mozzarella, Tomato & Basil; Ham & Cheese; Roast Beef & Cheese.

GIRLS ORNAMENT EXCHANGE

Hosting a Girl's Night is a great way to celebrate the holidays. Have everyone bring a gift-wrapped ornament to exchange. Have too many holiday ornaments? Exchange lipsticks, nail polish, etc. Once we select and open wrapped ornaments, one by one we go around the group and give each guest a chance to exchange—or keep the ornament opened. I can't tell you how many times the ornament I bought was traded for a different one. Anyway, lots of talking, catching up and laughter had by all!

MENU

Stinky Cheese & Ham Sandwiches *(page 144, the best ever sandwiches)*
Loaded Smashed Potatoes in individual martini glasses *(page 112)*
Bruschetta *(page 26)*
Shrimp Cocktail *(page 32)*
Artichoke Crab Jalapeño Dip *(page 49)*
Sugar's Toffee *(page 168)*

**Wine, Beer & Champagne
Vodka, of course,
and mixers.**

HOLIDAY BUS PARTY

No drinking & driving! The bus picks everyone up and arrives at the host/hostess house. Appetizers, food and cocktails for everyone along with holiday trivia and prizes. Then you are OFF on the bus to patronize a few establishments. Each passenger will receive a "munchie bag" containing:

MUNCHIE BAG

French Ham & Cheese Sandwich *(page 142)*
Potato Chips
Pickle
Chocolate Chip Cookie with Sea Salt *(page 156)*
Breath Mints
Bottle of Water
2 Aspirins

Appetizers

Appetizers are my favorite part of any meal. More times then not, they are the only part of my meals and family get-togethers as well. So do what we do– make 4 or 5 of these, put them out with small plates and call it DONE!

Fruit & Cheese Platter Bruschetta

Smoked Salmon Spicy Tuna Avocado

Pepperoncini Hummus Potato Skins

Shrimp Cocktail Carpaccio

Broiled Jalapeño, Cheese & Bacon Appetizer

Skewered Tortellini with Dipping Sauce

Guacamole Baked Tortilla Chips

Egg Salad Dip/Spread Stuffed Onions

French Roasted Vegetables Silky Chicken Liver Pate

Seared Scallops with Tartar Sauce

Artichoke Crab Jalapeño Dip

Anti-Pasta Platter Truffle Deviled Eggs

Crusty French Bread Crackers

Avocado Wedges Apple & Cheese Crostini

Mushroom & Brie Crostini Grilled Cheese

FRUIT & CHEESE PLATTER
SERVES 12-15

Offer both white and yellow wedges of cheese. Make sure to have at least one wedge of soft cheese like a St. Andre. Delicious!

Wedges of cheese
Large red grapes, apple and/or pear slices
Blackberries, nuts, strawberries, fresh figs
French bread crackers

Choose a selection of 4 or 5 hard and soft cheeses such as: white Wisconsin Cheddar, Gouda, Goat cheese, St. Andre soft cheese and Brie. Cheeses with fruit are also great choices, such as a white cheddar with cranberries.

I like to use large, round platters for this appetizer. Place assorted fruit in the center of the platter. Arrange the cheese, nuts and crackers around the fruit.

Make sure the soft cheeses have a small, rounded cheese knife and the hard cheeses have a small sharp knife.

BRUSCHETTA
SERVES 8-10

Bruschetta has a variety of ingredients. These are my personal favorites. Get creative and add or delete based on your tastes.

- 6 roma tomatoes, chopped – you can use heirloom or beefsteak tomatoes, just squeeze some of the seeds out
- 2 avocados, peeled and chopped
- 1 medium red onion, chopped
- 1 package Buffalo Mozzarella, cut into bite size pieces
- 1 cup Feta cheese, cut into bite size pieces
- 1 cup pitted kalamata olives, chopped
- 1 cup artichoke hearts, chopped
- Pan seared or boiled shrimp, cut into bite size pieces
- Olive oil
- Salt & pepper

Mix all vegetables, cheese and shrimp. Pour olive oil over mixture, using about 1/3 to 1/2 cup, tasting as you mix. Add salt and pepper to taste and carefully mix again.

This should be served at room temperature with crackers or tortilla chips.

SMOKED SALMON
SERVES 12

This is a favorite of mine. I love the thin, smoked salmon that can be purchased at most grocery stores. It is delicious dressed up with the below ingredients.

        1 package smoked salmon
        2 hard-boiled eggs, peeled and chopped
        1/2 red onion, chopped
        3 tablespoons capers
        Dijon mustard or other spicy mustard
        6 slices white bread, toasted and crusts removed or French bread crackers
        4 small ramekins *(optional)*

On a serving platter, arrange smoked salmon. Put each chopped ingredient - egg, onion, capers and mustard in a ramekin or simply scatter all over the salmon. Place long, thin serving forks on salmon and small knife/fork or spoons in ramekins.

Cut toasted bread into quarters or serve with French bread crackers. Add toast to platter, serve and enjoy!!

SPICY TUNA AVOCADO APPETIZER
SERVES 6

If you like tuna you will love this! This is even is better if refrigerated overnight. ALSO – the lime juice "cooks" the tuna some, so even if you don't love sushi, you will probably still love this. I serve this with French bread crackers and extra avocado to top tuna, if desired.

- 2 sushi-grade tuna steaks
- 2 avocados, peeled, pits removed, and chopped
- 3 green onions, chopped
- 1 large lime or 2 smaller limes
- 3 tablespoons wasabi powder
- 1/3 to 1/2 cup olive oil
- Salt & pepper

Cut tuna steaks into bite size pieces. Put tuna in a large bowl. Add avocado and chopped green onion to tuna.

Zest lime. Put zest in a separate bowl and squeeze lime juice over zest. Be sure to discard seeds. Add 1/3 cup olive oil to lime zest/juice. Sprinkle wasabi powder over olive oil mixture and combine well.

Pour olive oil mixture over tuna and gently mix thoroughly. Add additional olive oil if needed. Salt and pepper to taste.

Serve this fabulous tuna with French bread crackers. You will be asked for this recipe many, many times.

PEPPERONCINI HUMMUS
SERVES 12

Pepperoncini peppers are delicious on their own – and a simply delicious highlight to this very tasty hummus. I always serve this hummus with additional chopped pepperoncini and warm flatbread.

> **2 cans garbanzo beans, drained**
> **1/2 cup tahini**
> **2 tablespoons minced garlic**
> **1/4 cup olive oil**
> **1 teaspoon cayenne pepper**
> **1 cup chopped pepperoncini peppers**
> **1 teaspoon salt**

Combine all ingredients in a food processor. Process ingredients until hummus is smooth. Add additional olive oil if consistency is too thick. Garnish with chives and chopped tomatoes if desired. Serve with warm flatbread or panini pressed French bread and chopped pepperoncini peppers. Delicious!

POTATO SKINS
SERVES 12

Who doesn't love a potato skin. I have basic toppings, but feel free to get creative and top with what you like.

I bring these to football tailgates – I bake them in the morning and serve them at room temperature with toppings. They disappear quickly.

5 russet potatoes
1 pound shredded Sharp Cheddar cheese
8-10 pieces of bacon, cooked and crumbled (or more to taste)
Canola oil for frying

TOPPINGS
Chopped green onion, sour cream, salt & pepper, salsa

Preheat oven to 350 degrees. Wash potatoes and pierce in 5 or 6 places with a fork or a knife. Brush skins with olive oil. Place potatoes directly on oven rack and bake for about an hour. Once knife slides into potato easily, potatoes are done.

Cool potatoes completely. Cut potatoes length-wise and scoop out inside leaving a half inch potato skin. Reserve potato insides for another use.

Pour canola oil into a large skillet *(1 inch high)* and heat oil until smoking slightly. Place potato skins into pan so they fit comfortably – do not overcrowd. Fry potato skins for approximately 3-4 minutes on each side, turning with tongs. Once lightly brown on edges, remove from pan and place on paper towels to drain.

When all skins are fried, place potatoes on a cookie sheet and top each potato with crumbled bacon and shredded cheese.

Bake in preheated oven for about 25 minutes, until cheese is melted and bubbly. Remove from heat and serve with toppings.

SHRIMP COCKTAIL, WITH A TWIST
SERVES 6-8

This is always a big hit!

Buy an avocado that gives when squeezed but is not mushy.

2 pounds large shrimp, boiled with tails on – chilled
1 cup ketchup
1 haas avocado, peeled, pit removed and chopped into small chunks
3 tablespoons grated horseradish *(or more to taste)*
1/2 cup chopped red onion
Salt & pepper
Juice of 1/2 a lemon – or to taste

Put ketchup in medium bowl. Add avocado and remainder of ingredients. Mix well. Put in serving bowl, surround by shrimp and serve.

BROILED JALAPEÑO, CHEESE & BACON APPETIZER
SERVES 24

The combination of spicy, fresh jalapeños, melted cheese and salty, savory bacon is hard to resist. Yet another delicious small bite that can be served warm or at room temperature.

12 fresh jalapeños, sliced in half lengthwise, seeds removed
1 brick Monterey Jack cheese
24 slices bacon
Garlic salt & pepper

Preheat oven to low broil. Place cut jalapeños on broiler pan. Cut chunks of cheese to fit inside each cut jalapeño. Sprinkle with garlic salt – or plain salt if you prefer – and pepper.

Wrap each jalapeño half with a slice of bacon, covering entire jalapeño and cheese.

Place broiler pan in oven close to broiler heat. Broil approximately 7-8 minutes, checking often. Bacon should not be crispy, but cooked. If bacon is not cooked and cheese bubbling after 8 minutes, turn broiler to high for 1 minute or less (again, watching closely).

SKEWERED TORTELLINI WITH LEMON DIPPING SAUCE
SERVES 12

Super easy as you simply purchase the tortellini. Tasty and visually appealing.

1 package fresh cheese tortellini pasta
Long wooden skewers *(soaked for one hour)*
1 lemon
1 teaspoon minced garlic
1 cup plain yogurt
1 tablespoon chopped dill
Salt & pepper

Soak wooden skewers in water for one hour. Bring a large pot of water to a boil and add tortellini. Cook according to instructions.

While pasta is cooking, zest lemon. Put yogurt in a bowl and add lemon zest. Cut lemon in half and add juice, chopped dill and garlic. Mix well. Season with salt and pepper to taste and mix again.

Once pasta is done, drain water and cool. Once cool enough to handle, put 3 to 4 tortellini pieces on each wooden stick and put finished skewers in either a pretty glass or stacked on a serving platter. Serve skewered tortellini's with a small bowl of dipping sauce and enjoy!

GUACAMOLE
SERVES 4-6

Guacamole is one of the best foods ever. It is also healthy—just watch what foods you pair with your guacamole. It's also a wonderful substitute for mayonnaise on turkey, beef or chicken sandwiches.

If not serving right away, reserve several of the avocado pits and add to guacamole. The pits (along with citrus from the lime) prevent the avocado from turning black. Remove pits and stir guacamole before serving.

5 ripe *(not mushy)* **avocados, peeled, pitted and coarsely chopped**
1/2 to 2/3 cup red salsa, mild or hot *(optional)*
2 tablespoons fresh cilantro, minced
1 lime
1/3 cup red onion, chopped

Place chopped avocado into large bowl. If using, add 1/2 cup salsa, chopped red onion and cilantro to avocado and mix well. Squeeze the juice of one lime over guacamole mixture and stir thoroughly to combine.

Add additional salsa if desired. Serve with my tortilla chips (recipe to the right) or purchased chips. Love, love, love guac and baked chips. Enjoy!

BAKED TORTILLA CHIPS
SERVES 6-8

These are absolutely delicious – and not fried. So enjoy with your homemade guacamole, salsa, whatever!

2 packages flour tortillas
Olive oil
Sea Salt

Preheat broiler to low broil. Cut each tortillas into 6 or 8 pieces, depending on the size of chips you want. Place cut tortillas separately on a cookie sheet and brush with olive oil. Turn tortillas over and brush bottom with olive oil as well. Generously salt tortillas with sea salt.

Put cookie sheet in broiler on the top self. Cook chips for about 2 minutes. Watch chips closely as they will burn easily. Once lightly brown, take cookie sheet out and turn chips over. Put back in broiler and cook for another 1-2 minutes, watching closely. Remove from broiler after very lightly brown and cool. Continue with remaining tortillas until done. Cool chips completely and serve. These are light and happy chips. Enjoy!

Appetizers

EGG SALAD DIP/SPREAD
SERVES 12-14

Another family favorite. Served at most family functions and ALL football tailgates. This appetizer will disappear quickly. Somewhat – no VERY addictive. Sometimes I get kind of creative and shape this into a football, using green onions to form the football "laces." So easy and so good.

This is also great in the morning on a toasted bagel.

- **10 hard-boiled eggs, peeled and cooled**
- **2-1/2 8 ounce bricks reduced fat cream cheese, room temperature**
- **Approximately 1/2 cup reduced fat sour cream** *(more if you want the spread thinner)*
- **6 chopped green onions, greens included** *(plus long green onion pieces if shaping into a football)*
- **Garlic salt**
- **Salt & pepper**

Mix room temperature cream cheese and sour cream until thoroughly combined. Coarsely chop eggs. Add chopped eggs and green onion to cream cheese. Add garlic salt (7-8 shakes) and salt and pepper to taste. Gently mix until all ingredients are combined. Add extra garlic salt to taste.

Refrigerate until serving. Serve with crackers or French bread. Delicious!

CARPACCIO
SERVES 8-10

This is delicious and elegant. I like to use more expensive cuts of meat – even mignon – as it is all about the meat with this dish! **NOTE: Beef must be refrigerated for 48 hours, so begin 2 days prior to serving.**

- 1 pound fillet of beef, rinsed and patted dry
- 8-10 sprigs fresh thyme
- 8-10 sprigs fresh basil
- 8-10 sprigs fresh parsley
- 8-10 sprigs fresh tarragon
- 2 tablespoons coarse sea salt
- Wedge of Parmesan cheese, optional
- Olive oil
- Pepper

Lay half of the herbs in single row on a piece of foil large enough to cover the beef. Sprinkle herbs with 1 tablespoon of sea salt. Place beef on top of herbs. Line remaining herbs on top of the beef and sprinkle with 1 tablespoon of sea salt. Wrap foil tightly around the beef and place in the refrigerator - on a large plate, for 48 hours.

A couple of hours before serving, place wrapped beef in the freezer so slicing it is easier. When removed from freezer, unwrap the beef and remove herbs. Using the edge of a knife, scrap remaining herbs and salt off the beef.

Using a meat slicer – or a very sharp knife – cut the beef as thinly as possible.

Lay cut beef on a serving platter, overlapping the slices. Drizzle with olive oil and salt and pepper to taste. Shave Parmesan cheese (if using) over carpaccio and serve with warm crusty bread. Delicious!!!

STUFFED ONIONS
SERVES 6-8

This is a super cool and tasty dish that can be served as a "finger food" heavy appetizer, or a side dish to your entrée. These are terrific served with pasta or other meatless dishes. Excellent cocktail food too!

5-6 small red or white onions
2/3 pound ground beef or pork
1 cup bread crumbs
1/2 cup milk
2 tablespoons chopped fresh flat-leaf parsley
2 cloves minced garlic
2 eggs, beaten
Salt to taste
1/2 cup beef stock

Preheat oven to 350 degrees. Peel onions and cut a sliver off the bottoms so they can stand upright on a tray. Also, cut enough off the top to create a fairly wide opening, a little less than half. Boil onions in salted water about 10-15 minutes. Remove from water and set aside.

Reserve 2 teaspoons beaten egg and set aside. Combine meat, bread, parsley, garlic, milk and egg. Mix well.

Once the onions are cool enough to handle (don't want to burn the fingers!) scoop out the inner part. It can be difficult to hollow out the onions, so use a small knife to cut up the inside and scoop out with a spoon. Fill hollowed out onions with the meat mixture. If an onion begins to break while removing the insides, no worries. Simply press the onion around the meat mixture.

NOTE: If you don't want to discard the scooped inner part of the onion, you can combine it with your meat mixture.

Brush filled onions with reserved egg and top with salt.

Bake uncovered in a glass baking dish, basting with beef stock every 10 minutes. Bake for about 30 minutes. Serve on a tray for appetizers or as a side with an entrée.

FRENCH ROASTED VEGETABLES
SERVES 10-12

This is a wonderful appetizer and is served with either a ranch dressing or any kind of creamy dressing – homemade or purchased.

2 large red onions or 4 smaller onions
2 yellow squash
2 zucchini
4 roma tomatoes or 2 beefsteak tomatoes
2 red or yellow bell peppers
8 small red potatoes
10 large mushrooms, whole
Olive oil
Salt & pepper

Preheat oven to 475 degrees. Thoroughly wash all vegetables and pat dry.

Slice red potatoes in half and put on cookie sheet. Sprinkle with about 3 tablespoons olive oil and mix to coat. Salt and pepper potatoes.

Put potatoes in oven for 15 minutes. While potatoes are cooking, slice red onions crosswise in half, leaving skins on.

Slice peppers into quarters, removing seeds. Cut squash and zucchini into 1 inch chunks, discarding ends. Cut tomatoes crosswise in half. Leave mushrooms whole unless they are very large – then cut in half lengthwise.

In bowl, combine all vegetables but potatoes and toss in 6-7 tablespoons olive oil. Remove potatoes from oven and put all vegetables, including potatoes, on the cookie sheet in one layer – do not overlap. Make sure all veggies are cut side down.

Salt and pepper veggies and cook in preheated oven for about 30 minutes. Veggies should be wrinkled and soft and knife should pierce potatoes easily

Place all veggies on a large serving platter and put a small bowl of dipping sauce in the middle. Again, a great finger food – although you may want to cut the onions into smaller pieces.

SEARED SCALLOPS WITH TARTAR SAUCE
SERVES 15-20

This is a wonderful dish that is simply a causal twist on the delicious scallop we love so much. It is perfect for a cocktail party – or any party that focuses on finger food. No worries about serving without utensils – these are OK to pick up with your fingers. Just make sure you have cocktail napkins close by. You will want a small spoon in the tartare sauce for those who want to spoon the sauce on their scallops.

Scallops are quite tasty hot AND and at room temperature!

2 – 2 1/2 pounds large scallops
Olive oil
Salt & pepper
Garlic salt
Panko crumbs (optional)

Thoroughly rinse scallops under cool water and set aside. Pour several tablespoons of olive oil in a non-stick pan and heat to medium high heat – until oil in pan is sizzling.

If using panko, put panko in a wide-bottomed bowl and dip each flat side of the scallops in the panko (they will still be wet and panko will adhere) and carefully place scallops in hot pan – spacing an inch or two apart. Scallops should not touch as it will inhibit cooking. If not using panko, simply place scallops in hot pan.

Cook scallops for approximately two minutes. Turn scallops over and cook for another minute or so. You can cut one scallop in half to make sure they are cooked to your preference – and remember they will continue cooking briefly once off heat.

Place cooked scallops on large platter, leaving space in the center of the platter for a small bowl of tartar sauce.

TARTAR SAUCE
1 cup reduced fat mayonnaise
2 tablespoons reduced fat sour cream
5 tablespoons capers, plus 1 teaspoon caper juice
5 tablespoons finely chopped red onion

Combine all ingredients, mix well and place in a small bowl. Arrange scallops around bowl of sauce and serve!

SILKY CHICKEN LIVER PATE
SERVES 20-25

My good friend Lisa gave me this recipe. (An aside: She was supposed to write this cookbook with me but BAILED). Her mother has been making this since she was a kid. She recently brought it to one of our many parties and I was immediately hooked! I love pate and really love this. Years ago Lisa's mom got this recipe from a Dinah Shore cookbook and has been slowly changing and tweaking ever since—most likely forgetting ingredients so adding what she thought would work. It definitely works! **NOTE: This needs 24 hours in refrigerator.**

1 pound chicken livers
2 medium onions, chopped
3/4 cup butter
1 garlic clove, crushed
1 tablespoon flour
1/4 teaspoon sugar
1 teaspoon salt
1/2 teaspoon pepper
1 bay leaf
Pinch thyme, oregano and tarragon
3 tablespoons brandy
Clarified butter, to cover pate if desired

Sauté onions and garlic in 1/2 cup butter. Cook over medium heat until tender, approximately 6 minutes. Transfer onion and garlic to bowl and set aside. Melt 1/4 cup butter in skillet and sauté chicken livers until tender, 8-10 minutes. Sprinkle livers with flour and stir in thyme, oregano, tarragon, sugar, bay leaf, salt and pepper. Cover skillet and simmer for 2-4 minutes over very low heat. Remove bay leaf.

Cool mixture. Once cool, add onions and garlic. Add brandy. In batches, puree pate in food processor until completely smooth. Once pate is pureed, spoon into a crock and cover with clarified butter (if using). Cover crock and refrigerate until serving – at least 24 hours.

ANTI-PASTA PLATTER
SERVES 12

You can get creative with this and add different types of vegetables, meats and cheeses. Add or delete anything you want to reflect your taste preferences. Go crazy!

    1/2 pound thinly sliced ham
    1/2 pound thinly sliced salami
    1 brick Sharp Cheddar cheese, sliced
    1 brick Jalapeño White Cheddar cheese, sliced
    1 brick Feta cheese, cut into bite size pieces
    Kalamata olives, pepperoncini peppers, small marinated onions and mushrooms from olive bar or purchase individually
    1 jar mini pickles

Using a large serving platter, combine all ingredients. If you are a strict personality and like things in "order," create rows of each item, alternating meats, cheeses and vegetables. If you like to wing it, create jumbled piles of each ingredient, overlapping/mixing the meats, cheese and vegetables together.

Drizzle anti-pasta with some extra virgin olive oil & sprinkle with salt & pepper. Serve this with some crackers and enjoy!!

ARTICHOKE CRAB JALAPEÑO DIP (HOT!)
SERVES 6-8

By now I'm sure we've all had the good ol' artichoke dip appetizer. To put a twist on it, add jalapeños and crab meat. Serve with bowl of your favorite tortilla chips or crackers. I am asked for this recipe all the time. Great tailgate/football food!

- **1 cup mayonnaise**
- **1–1 1/2 cups grated Parmesan cheese**
- **1/2 cup chopped green onion**
- **1/2 cup chopped jalapeño**
- **2 cans artichoke hearts, drained** *(13 ounce)*
- **2 small containers** *(or 1 large container)* **chunk crab meat**

Preheat oven to 400 degrees. Using a kitchen scissors or a knife, cut artichokes into quarters or smaller. In bowl, mix all ingredients. Put into an oven-safe serving dish and top with seasoned breadcrumbs. Drizzle with olive oil. Bake for 35-40 minutes until top turns brown and dip bubbles a bit. Cool slightly and serve!

TRUFFLE DEVILED EGGS
SERVES 12-15

Deviled eggs are easy to prepare and most people love them. I absolutely love all things truffle and use both truffle oil and truffle salt in these.

12 hard-boiled eggs, peeled
1/2 to 3/4 cup mayonnaise
3 tablespoons spicy mustard
2 tablespoons white truffle oil
Truffle salt
6 green onions, chopped

Cut all eggs in half lengthwise and scoop out yolks and put in a bowl. Set whites aside. Using a fork, mash all yolks until smooth. Add mayonnaise and mustard. Mix until all ingredients are completely incorporated. Add truffle oil and 1 teaspoon of truffle salt. Mix thoroughly.

If you have piping instruments, use these to pipe yolk mixture onto egg whites. If you don't have a "piper," you can take a plastic Ziploc bag, spoon yolk mixture into the bag and cut one of the corners of the bag. Be sure to cut just a small portion of the bag. Squeeze from the top of the bag and the yolk mixture will "pipe" onto the egg whites.

Lightly sprinkle eggs with additional truffle salt and chopped green onion and serve! If not serving within an hour, refrigerate until ready to serve.

APPLE CHEESE CROSTINI
SERVES 12-15

A tasty combination of salty and sweet. You'll want to eat ALL of these.

1 loaf Italian bread, sliced into 3/4 inch slices
Butter
Apple slices *(preferably Honey Crisp apples – they are by FAR the best)*
Slices of Monterey Jack cheese *(one for each slice of bread)*
Salt

Preheat oven to low broil. Butter both sides of Italian bread. Heat large frying pan and grill BOTH sides of the Italian bread.

Remove from pan and put each grilled piece of bread on a cookie sheet. Salt each piece of grilled bread. Cover bread with apple slices and put piece of cheese on top of apple.

Salt the top of apple/cheese crostini. Place under broiler until cheese is melted and bubbly (3-4 minutes or longer). Serve and enjoy!!!

CRUSTY FRENCH BREAD CRACKERS
SERVES 12

I always keep them on hand and store them in large Ziploc bags in the pantry. You will use these with many different dips and salads. They taste great and stay fresh for weeks.

One or two loaves of French bread
Olive oil
Salt, if desired

Preheat broiler to low. Cut loaves into 1/2 inch slices. Place cut bread on cookie sheet and sprinkle lightly with olive oil. Broil (WATCH CLOSELY) until light brown. Flip bread over and broil other side (2-3 minutes or so—do not walk away crackers will burn). Remove from oven, cool completely and store in Ziploc bags.

MUSHROOM & BRIE CROSTINI (AND VERSION 2, DECONSTRUCTED)
SERVES 12

The savory combination of mushrooms and Brie cheese can be served either hot out of the oven (which is how I usually eat them, but I suggest you actually take them out of the oven first) or at room temperature (much safer).

Put wedge of Brie in the freezer. It will slice much easier when a little hard. You can cut the skin off the Brie if desired, however it is great left on as well.

Crusty French bread crackers
One container each button mushrooms, baby bella mushrooms and shitake mushrooms
Olive oil
3 tablespoons chopped garlic
One large white onion, chopped
Chopped parsley, 2-3 tablespoons
Large wedge of your favorite Brie or other soft cheese

Preheat oven to 400 degrees. Place sliced bread on a cookie sheet, brush lightly with oil and bake until bread is lightly toasted, about 5-7 minutes. Take out of the oven and set aside. Wash and cut mushrooms into thin slices.

VERSION 1
Put about 3 tablespoons of olive oil in a large non-stick frying pan. Heat oil and add chopped onion. Sauté for about 3-4 minutes. Add chopped garlic. Sauté another 2 minutes. Add all mushrooms and mix well. Sauté until mushrooms are cooked through, about 5-7 minutes. Add more olive oil if it seems a bit dry. Add parsley and mix. Remove from heat. Put mixture on each cracker and top with a piece of Brie (trim Brie to fit on cracker).

Cook in preheated oven until Brie is melted, approximately 10 minutes. Remove from oven and serve. These are terrific hot or room temperature, so no worries about this appetizer cooling off.

VERSION 2
Sauté all above and remove from heat. Cut Brie into bite size pieces and add to the mushroom onion mixture. Cook over medium-low heat, stirring until cheese has melted. Remove from heat, spoon mixture onto individual appetizer plates or bowls, surround with crusty crackers, serve and enjoy!

OH SO TASTY GRILLED CHEESE WITH GRILLED FRENCH BREAD
SERVES 4-6 PER CHEESE SQUARE

This is another appetizer that is quick and easy – no actual "cooking" required! Just buy the cheese, grill it and the bread and you are a hero. This is requested a LOT. NOTE: I use a panini maker to grill both the bread and the cheese. If you don't have a panini maker you can use a cast iron grill pan.

Brunkow's baked cheese is available in most gourmet grocery stores. It comes in a variety of flavors. I like the jalapeño and garlic flavors best.

1 Brunkow's baked cheese in desired flavor
1 French baguette
Olive oil

Cut French bread length-wise. Brush each side lightly with olive oil. Cut French bread halves into 5 inch pieces to grill.

Heat panini maker to highest level. Place several pieces of bread cut side down on panini maker and close. Push hard on top handle to create grill marks. Cook about 3 minutes, keeping weight on panini handle.

If using cast iron skillet, heat skillet on high until smoking. Place bread cut side down on skillet and cover with a smaller heavy lid or smaller pot bottom, using weight to push down on bread.

Cook remaining bread and rip into smaller serving sizes. Put all bread on a serving platter.

Bring panini machine or skillet back up to high temperature. Place cheese on panini grill or skillet and close lid. Push hard on lid to again (or pot bottom), create grill marks. Let cheese cook for about 3 minutes. Cheese is done when it is somewhat melted and soft throughout, but still in one piece.

Put cheese on platter with bread. Place a small, appetizer knife next to cheese and serve. Absolutely delicious!

Appetizers 57

AVOCADO WEDGES
SERVES 6

This is a visually beautiful appetizer that is healthy and delicious.

4 ripe avocados, peeled, pitted and cut into wedges
Olive oil
1 lemon, cut into quarters
Fresh shaved Parmesan cheese
1 loaf ciabatta or French bread

Preheat oven to 350 degrees. Place unwrapped bread in oven and warm for about 20 minutes, until the crust is crispy and hot.

Arrange avocado slices on a plate and drizzle olive oil over avocado. Cut warm bread into 2 inch slices and arrange next to avocado slices. Shave fresh Parmesan over avocado and serve with lemon wedges.

NOTE: If not serving immediately, squeeze lemon over avocado to prevent browning. Also make sure you have a small, round cheese knife as the avocado can be spread on the bread slices.

SECOND VERSION
Heat up panini machine to hot. Cut bread in half length-wise. Brush cut side with oil or butter. Cut bread into lengths that fit into panini machine. Place 2 pieces in panini and close, pressing down very firmly. Hold closed until "beeper" sounds. Remove, spread avocado on panini "toast," drizzle with extra olive oil and lemon if desired and enjoy!

Chilis, Soups Salads & Stews

I decided to group these dishes together. While both warm bowl meals and salads can be terrific stand alone entrées, many are fabulous when paired. Hot and cold play well together. So get creative – mix & match!

French Onion Soup
Corn & Crab Chowder
Cream of Broccoli Soup
Chili Con Carne
Pumpkin Soup
Stuffed Pumpkin Soup
Classic Beef Stew
Larry's Chicken Chili
Arugula & Spinach Salad
Salad Niciose
Fresh Tuna Salad
Cranberry Tuna Salad
Bean & Kale Kick Ass Salad
Red Cabbage Cole Slaw
White Bean Salad
Fresh Corn & Tomato Salad

FRENCH ONION SOUP
SERVES APPROXIMATELY 8

I learned how to make French onion soup in a cooking class. It was delicious, but when I first made it at home, I thought I had dry sherry or white wine, but had neither. So I used marsala and liked the result so much, I've continued using marsala instead of dry sherry or white wine.

- 5 cups thinly sliced **white or yellow onions**
- 3 tablespoons unsalted butter
- 1 tablespoon vegetable oil
- 1 teaspoon salt
- 1 tablespoon sugar *(helps brown onions)*
- 4 tablespoons all **purpose flour**
- 2 quarts beef stock
- 1/2 cup marsala
- Salt & pepper
- 1 loaf crusty, day old **French bread sliced 2 inches thick, and toasted**
- 12 thick slices Swiss cheese, 2 slices cut into small pieces

Preheat oven to 375 degrees. Put beef stock in large, deep pot and warm stock on a medium high heat. While stock is warming, heat butter and oil in a heavy saucepan. Once butter and oil are heated, add sliced onions. Cover and cook on low heat for about 15 minutes.

Uncover, raise heat to medium and stir in salt and sugar. Cook for 35-40 minutes, stirring constantly until onions are a deep, golden brown. Sprinkle the 4 tablespoons flour over onions and stir for several minutes.

Add onions to beef stock and salt and pepper to taste. Add marsala and stir. Simmer partially covered for about 40 minutes and add seasoning to taste. Bring soup to boil.

While soup is heating up, place a few pieces of cut up Swiss cheese in oven-proof soup bowls. Pour soup into each bowl and put toasted bread on top of soup. Cover bread with Swiss cheese. You may need a bit more than one piece of cheese, so use it– you're covered!

Place soup bowls in oven for about 20 minutes – then put oven on high-broiler for a few minutes until cheese is bubbling. Remove from oven and serve immediately.

CORN & CRAB CHOWDER
SERVES 8

The chefs at the Tarpon Lodge on Pine Island, Florida, were gracious enough to share this fantastic recipe with me. I made a few changes – using half & half and skim milk instead of heavy cream (gotta fit into my bathing suit) and I doubled the amount of crab meat...of course.

NOTE: If you want the chowder to be thicker, add two tablespoons of cornstarch while heating prior to serving. For best results, let chowder sit on the stove on low simmer, uncovered for an hour or two prior to serving.

1 white or yellow onion, chopped
3 celery stalks, chopped
2 large cans white lump crab meat
1 teaspoon thyme
3/4 cup sherry *(not cooking sherry, but real sherry),* **extra to top soup cups**
1/2 gallon skim milk
4 cups half & half
2 cans corn – or 5 ears fresh corn, uncooked
3 tablespoons butter
6 tablespoons all purpose flour

In a large frying pan over medium heat, sauté onions and celery in butter until soft and translucent, about 6-7 minutes. Set aside. In deep soup pot, combine sherry, milk, half & half, corn and thyme. Salt & pepper to taste. Add crab meat and sautéed celery and onion. Heat until boiling, then reduce heat to medium.

In frying pan used to sauté onions, melt 3 tablespoons butter and add flour. Mix to form a roux (a thickening agent for soup), adding butter and/or flour as needed. Add roux to pot. Continue cooking over medium heat for about 15 minutes.

When ready to serve, fill soup bowls and drizzle a small amount of sherry on top of chowder (or a lot depending on what kind of day you're having).

CREAM OF BROCCOLI SOUP
SERVES 6

I love cream-based soups and this is my go-to recipe. Fresh or frozen broccoli can be used. I try to use fresh, but frozen can be a better option during the winter season. Once again, this hearty soup can be a full, satisfying meal.

4 cups fresh broccoli florets or 3 packages frozen packages
1 large yellow or white onion, chopped
2-1/2 cups skim milk *(or whole, 2%, whatever you desire)*
1-1/2 cups shredded Cheddar cheese – or Velveeta cheese, cubed
9 tablespoons flour
3 cans vegetable broth
6 tablespoons butter

TOPPINGS
Croûtons
Shredded Cheddar cheese
Sour cream

Put vegetable broth in a large pot and heat to a low boil. Add broccoli and maintain low boil for about 10 minutes.

In a separate skillet, melt 4 tablespoons butter over medium heat. Add chopped onion and sauté until translucent, about 5 minutes. Remove onions from pan and add to broccoli. Melt remaining butter over medium-low heat in the same pan, add the flour, stirring to form a roux (a thickening agent for soup). Cook until roux is light golden brown. Add flour and butter to the roux as needed.

Gradually add the milk, stirring constantly until well combined and thickens, 3-5 minutes. Add milk to broccoli and stir until smooth and combined. Add the cheese, stirring until melted. Salt and pepper to taste.

To serve, top each bowl of soup with a handful of shredded Cheddar cheese, croûtons, and a dollop of sour cream. Delicious and really filling…in a good way.

CHILI CON CARNE
SERVES 10-12

This is my favorite chili recipe. I'm not as fond of chili made with ground beef. This has two kinds of meat and fabulous toppings. Topping are very important. Offer many different kinds of toppings as everyone has unique tastes. Not a one-size fits all kind of meal.

2 -1/2 pounds chuck beef steak or a combination of beef and pork
   (Pork chops are my favorite)
2 white or yellow onions, chopped
2 small cans chilies, drained and chopped *(I use serrano and poblano)*
1 teaspoon cumin
2 tablespoons chopped garlic
4 tomatoes, chopped
1 16 ounce can chopped tomatoes
2 bottles of your favorite beer
Salt and cayenne pepper
Bay leaf
Olive oil

TOPPINGS
Chopped green onions
Sour cream
Shredded Cheddar cheese
Sliced avocado
Tortilla chips or Frito's
Sliced jalapeños
Cilantro

In a large non-stick skillet, brown all meat, scraping up brown bits with a wooden spoon. Transfer browned meat to a large chili pot and cover to keep warm. In the same skillet, sauté chopped onion and garlic in olive oil until soft.

Finely chop chilies and add to onions, continuing to sauté over a low heat for a few minutes. Add onion mixture, tomatoes, beer, cumin and bay leaf to meat. Bring chili to a boil, stirring. Lower heat to medium-high and stir. Simmer, stirring occasionally for about 2 hours. Adjust seasoning – add salt, cayenne or regular pepper to intensify heat.

Before serving, discard bay leaf. Serve chili in bowls and garnish with desired toppings.

PUMPKIN SOUP
SERVES 4

I absolutely love Fall – and the seasonal food is no exception. I love pumpkins and I love pumpkin soup! This is so very tasty – and can be served in individual small pumpkins or one large pumpkin shell. Cut an opening in the pumpkin (or pumpkins) and scoop out seeds, etc. until clean. Rinse in warm water, washing the inside and outside and set aside.

A 3 pound pumpkin should give you about 2 cups pumpkin meat.

If desired, cooked, chopped bacon can be added to soup. Add along with the milk and heat up.

4 small pumpkins, hollowed or one large pumpkin, hollowed
3 cups fresh pumpkin "meat," cut into 1 inch or so chunks
2 white onions, chopped
2 tablespoons chopped garlic
Finely grated rind – and juice of one orange
3 tablespoons olive oil
3 tablespoons fresh thyme, stalks removed and chopped
2/3 cup 2% milk
6 cups vegetable stock
2 tablespoons cornstarch

Preheat oven to 350 degrees. To cook hollowed out pumpkins, place the large pumpkin, or 4 small pumpkins, on a large cookie sheet or casserole dish lined with parchment paper. Place in preheated oven and cook for 1 hour. If pumpkin insides and skin can be pierced easily with a knife or fork, remove from oven and cool. If not, continue cooking and check every 15 minutes. Depending on the size/shape of the pumpkin(s), it can cook in an hour or take up to 2 hours to fully cook.

Set cooked pumpkins aside. In a large soup pot, heat olive oil. Add chopped onions and cook over medium heat until softened, about 3-4 minutes. Add garlic and chopped pumpkin meat. Cook for another 3-4 minutes, stirring constantly.

Add vegetable stock, orange rind and juice to pan. Simmer over medium low heat for 10 minutes. Add 2 tablespoons thyme and continue simmering for another 10 minutes or until the pumpkin pieces are tender.

Remove from heat and cool slightly. Puree mixture in a food processor or use a hand processor. Blend until smooth. Season with salt and pepper to taste.

Return soup to pot, add milk and cornstarch. Heat until boiling. Reduce heat and simmer until thickened, about 10 minutes. Pour the soup into the cooked pumpkins, top with remaining tablespoon thyme. Not only tasty, but beautiful as well. Serve with hot, crusty bread and enjoy.

NOTE: Be sure to scrape the walls of the pumpkin "soup bowl" while eating to add extra pumpkin meat to your soup. It's delicious and adds a tasty "plus" to an already terrific dish.

STUFFED PUMPKINS
SERVES 4

This is another way to serve pumpkins in the fall. They really are made for more than just carving – they are delicious and such a stunning presentation. This recipe is something else that can be altered to suit your taste buds. I first found this in another cook book and have added and deleted items so many times I really can't remember the original version….you should do the same. Note: Rip baguette into pieces and leave out, uncovered overnight. You can use half & half or whole milk in place of skim milk if preferred.

4 small orange pumpkins, cleaned, shelled and lids saved
1 stale French baguette, ripped into bite sized pieces one day prior to serving
1/2 pound Gruyère cheese *(or your favorite hard cheese),* **cut into cubes**
1 large yellow or white onion, chopped
1 tablespoon thyme
1/2 cup *(plus extra to top)* **skim milk**
2 cups mushrooms, button or portabella
6 strips cooked bacon or prosciutto, chopped *(optional)*
1/2 pound ground beef, browned *(optional)*
2 cups small yellow potatoes, chopped into 1 inch pieces
2 teaspoon chopped garlic
Salt & pepper

Preheat oven to 375 degrees. Line two cookie sheets with parchment paper and set aside. In a large bowl, mix bread, onion, bacon and ground beef (if using), mushrooms, cheese, potatoes, garlic and spices. Toss until mixed. Add 1/2 cup skim milk and toss to combine.

Place pumpkins on covered cookie sheets and pack each with bread mixture. Once packed, pour extra skim milk over each. About 1/4 cup. Pierce the skin of each pumpkin with a fork or knife in 4 or 5 places. Put the tops back on each pumpkin and bake for about 1 hour 15 minutes. Check pumpkins. If the flesh cannot be pierced easily, continue baking. It may take another half hour or so. Once flesh can be pierced and the inside is nice and bubbling hot, pumpkins are about done. Now remove lids and bake another 5 minutes or so to "crust" the tops.

Remove from oven and plate each pumpkin with the lid slightly off-center to expose the beautiful feast inside. A small salad prior to this main course is all you need to make this a stunning and memorable meal.

Remind your guest to "dig into" the pumpkin flesh while eating. The pumpkin meat along with the stuffing, makes for an amazing food "party" in your mouth!

CLASSIC BEEF STEW
SERVES 6

Here is another terrific slow cooker meal, although this can be slow cooked in a heavy stew pot on the stove as well. Once again this has the traditional stew ingredients, but can be altered based on personal tastes. Chris and I do not like cooked carrots and so I usually leave them out – unless I am making this for a group. Feel free to improvise!

Beef stew meat can be found already cut at most grocery stores. If not, your butcher can cut it to your specifications. Also, if not using some of the above vegetables, simply increase the amount of the vegetables you are using.

2 pounds beef stew meat, cut into 1 inch cubes
4 golden potatoes, skins on, cut into 1 inch cubes
1 large yellow onion, chopped into 1 inch pieces
1 tablespoon minced garlic
3 carrots, cut into 1 inch pieces
1/2 cup celery *(optional)*
2 cups beef broth
1/2 cup red wine *(optional)*
1/2 cup all purpose flour
1 tablespoon salt
1 tablespoon pepper
2 tablespoons olive oil
1 teaspoon paprika
1 bay leaf

Heat olive oil in a large non-stick pan. Put flour, paprika, salt and pepper in a medium bowl. Dredge meat cubes in flour and shake off the excess. Brown meat in the pan. Do not crowd meat or it will not cook, but "steam." Be sure to brown all sides. Once brown, remove from pan. Put slow cooker on a medium-low setting. Place browned meat into the slow cooker (or large stew pot). Scrape up browned bits in pan and add to meat in the cooker.

Add all other ingredients and stir to mix. Cover cooker or pot and cook for 2 hours, stirring occasionally with a wooden spoon. Be sure to scrape up bits on the bottom. After 2 hours, lower heat to low and continue cooking for 3 hours or up to 6 hours, checking, stirring and scraping occasionally.

When done, all you need is some warm, crusty bread and it's a hearty, delicious meal! Leftovers are fabulous too. Just reheat and enjoy.

LARRY'S CHICKEN CHILI
SERVES 4

This is my brother-in-law Larry's recipe. Excellent and easy. Feel free to add or delete spices based on how hot you want the chili to be. I like a super spicy chili and add accordingly.

- 2 cans diced tomatoes with jalapeño, not drained
- 2 cans black beans with lime, not drained
- 2 cooked chicken breasts, skin removed, chicken deboned and pulled apart into bite size pieces
- 1 can light beer
- Salt & pepper

TOPPINGS FOR CHILI
- 1 chopped white onion
- 1 cup shredded Cheddar cheese
- Sour cream
- 1 avocado, chopped
- Additional chopped jalapeños
- Tortilla chips or Frito's

In a large soup pan, combine tomatoes with juice, beans with juice, chicken and beer. Bring mixture to boil and then reduce heat. Simmer on low for approximately 45 minutes.

Serve with toppings and enjoy!

Larry Miller

ARUGULA/SPINACH SALAD WITH KALAMATA OLIVES AND PARMESAN-REGGIANO CHEESE
SERVES 4

I love the spicy taste of arugula and sometimes just snack on the leaves. Great little bite. When combined with cheese and olives, it is irresistible.

> **1 bunch arugula, washed and stemmed**
> **4 cups fresh spinach**
> **20-25 kalamata olives, halved**
> **1/2 red onion, thinly sliced**
> **CGD: Crazy Good Dressing** *(If not available use olive oil and salad vinegar)*
> **Wedge Parmesan-Reggiano cheese**
> **Lemon wedge**
> **Salt & pepper**
> **Pecans or walnuts** *(optional)*

If not using CGD, in a medium bowl combine approximately 1/4 cup olive oil and 8-10 shakes salad vinegar. Whisk thoroughly. Add more olive oil or vinegar to taste. When satisfied with oil/vinegar mixture, add salt & pepper and a squeeze of the lemon wedge. Whisk to combine.

Put arugula and spinach in large bowl, pour dressing over and toss well to coat arugula. Season with salt and pepper. Add red onion and toss again.

Divide salad between four salad plates or bowls. Top each salad with olives. With a cheese shaver, shave cheese on each salad and top with nuts, if using.

SALAD NICOISE
SERVES 2

As you have probably figured out, I adore most things French (especially young French men), and the infamous French version of tuna salad is no exception. Serve as a delicious and healthy lunch or dinner along with a fabulous warm, crusty baguette and I assure you, this will not disappoint.

Any type of fresh green bean will work – however if your grocery carries haricots verts (French beans) these are the best.

1 pouch or can albacore tuna *(drained if using canned)*
8 ounces *(1/2 pound)* **green beans, washed with stems trimmed**
2 hard-boiled eggs, peeled and cut into quarters
3 tablespoons capers
1/3 cup pitted kalamata olives, sliced lengthwise
2 crosswise thin slices red onion, cut in quarters
1 bunch arugula
1/2 ripe *(but still semi-firm)* **avocado, cut into 1 inch chunks**
4 to 6 small red potatoes, washed

This dressing is a very tasty, light lemony addition to any salad and is a wonderful dipping sauce for vegetables. I always soak up any leftover salad dressing with baguettes. Delicious!

DRESSING
3 tablespoons dijon mustard
1 lemon, juiced
1/3 to 1/2 cup high quality olive oil
1 teaspoon salt
1 teaspoon pepper
1/2 teaspoon garlic powder or crushed fresh garlic

Bring a pot of water to a boil and add washed/trimmed green beans. Cook until beans are tender, but still crisp, approximately 5 minutes. A fork should pierce green beans fairly easily. Once cooked, drain green beans and place in a bowl of ice water to stop cooking and chill.

Cut red potatoes into quarters. Do not peel potatoes. In same pot, add water and boil until potatoes are tender and can be pierced with a fork– approximately 8 minutes. Drain potatoes and set aside. While beans and potatoes are cooling, prepare salad dressing. Combine mustard, lemon and spices together and whisk until well combined. While whisking constantly, drizzle 1/3 cup olive oil until incorporated. Taste dressing and add additional oil if desired. Adjust spices accordingly.

Cut green beans in half. In large bowl, combine arugula, green beans, sliced onion, 2 tablespoons capers, olives and mix until combined. Add tuna, potatoes and avocado. Pour dressing over (reserving a few tablespoons) and carefully mix until all ingredients are combined. Divide salad into 2 large salad bowls. Top each salad with quartered eggs and 1 tablespoon capers. Drizzle remaining dressing on top. Serve with warmed baguette and voila! A fabulous, healthy meal.

FRESH TUNA SALAD
SERVES 2

You may never eat canned tuna again.

This tastes wonderful on crusty French bread. But what doesn't?

1 fresh tuna steak
1 cup *(or more)* **light mayonnaise**
1/2 red onion, chopped
3 tablespoons wasabi powder
Salt & pepper
Olive oil
1/2 cup capers, optional

Drizzle olive oil over tuna steak and sprinkle with salt and pepper. Either broil tuna until cooked through or grill 4-5 minutes. Turn tuna and grill another 4-5 minutes until cooked through.

Cool completely. Flake tuna with fork and add all ingredients. Gently mix together until combined. Serve immediately or chill.

Chili's, Soups, Salads & Stews

CRANBERRY TUNA SALAD
SERVES 2

This is my version of the delicious tuna salad with cranberries from Whole Foods.

- **2 cans white meat tuna in pouches or cans, drained** (*or 2 fresh tuna steaks, cooked through, cooled and flaked*)
- **1/2 to 3/4 cup light mayonnaise**
- **4 green onions, chopped**
- **1/2 cup dried cranberries** (*the reduced sugar version is the best*) – **more if desired.**
- **1 teaspoon salt**
- **1/2 to 1 teaspoon cayenne pepper**
- **1 tablespoon olive oil**

Mix all ingredients. Chill until an hour before serving. Serve as an appetizer with crackers, or with rolls or bread for sandwiches.

BEAN AND KALE KICK ASS SALAD
SERVES 5

My fabulous daughter Molly brought me to a Chipotle restaurant for lunch when I was visiting her at Saint Mary's College, South Bend, Indiana. My (apparently incorrect) view of Chipotle was that everything on the menu was fat-laden and grossly unhealthy. Well, I didn't know about the salad line where I can choose everything that goes into my salad. The good, the bad and the ugly was all dictated by me. Well, I ended up with a salad full of protein and healthy fat. Crazy good. As soon as I got home, I created MY version of the crazy good salad, topping it off with my Crazy Good Dressing (GCD). I eat this often and if I stick with this as my dinner entrée for about 2 weeks, I lose 8-10 pounds without even trying. Give it a go – you won't be disappointed.

It serves 5, but I use it just for me for 5 days. It keeps for about a week in the fridge and each day I add more fresh kale for the vitamins and the crunch.

* Marconi is the BEST. I love the hot version, but you can play it safe and get the mild version.

1 bunch kale, washed and ripped into bite size pieces
1 avocado, chopped
2 roma tomatoes, chopped
3 green onions, chopped
1 can black beans, drained and rinsed
1 can chickpeas *(garbanzo beans)* **drained and rinsed**
1 can white beans, drained and rinsed
1 cup spicy Italian veggies – Marconi, Hot Giardiniera (drained)*
1 cup baked tofu, optional
Salt & pepper
1 teaspoon cayenne pepper *(optional)*
1/2 cup Susan's CGD: Crazy Good Dressing to taste *(If you didn't buy my dressing, use your favorite Italian. It won't be as good as mine, but it'll do I guess).*

OPTIONAL INGREDIENTS
Quinoa
Chopped lean chicken or steak
Chopped red cabbage – excellent addition as it maintains its crunch

Super easy to construct. Simply combine all ingredients but the CGD. Mix well. Now add CGD to your taste and thoroughly combine. Amazing flavors and completely guilt-free. How often can you say that?

Cover the left-overs and put in the refrigerator. Add kale and meat, if desired, daily and your dinner is done.

Chili's, Soups, Salads & Stews 85

RED CABBAGE COLESLAW
SERVES 8-10

This is a terrific lighter version of the traditional coleslaw-swimming-in-mayo. Light, crisp flavor. The caraway seeds are a MUST.

Cabbage and onion can be sliced thinly with a meat slicer.

1 head red cabbage, thinly sliced and chopped into approximately 1 inch pieces
3 large lemons
3 tablespoons caraway seeds
3/4 cup light mayonnaise
1 thinly sliced red onion
1-1/2 teaspoon salt
2 teaspoons pepper

Place thinly sliced cabbage and onion in a large bowl. Add mayonnaise, salt and pepper and mix well.

Slice lemons in half and squeeze juice into cabbage mixture (wrapping lemon halves in cheesecloth will ensure no seeds escape into coleslaw). Mix well.

Add 3 tablespoons caraway seeds to cabbage and toss well to thoroughly combine all ingredients. Give the slaw several hours to blend flavors prior to serving, or refrigerate overnight. Remove from refrigerator an hour prior to serving.

This is delicious as a side and as a topping on pulled pork or chicken sandwiches.

WHITE BEAN SALAD
SERVES 4

Beans are not only very healthy, but also quite tasty, as this salad will prove.

2 cans cannellini beans, drained
1/2 red onion, chopped
3 plum tomatoes, chopped
1/3 cup chopped Italian parsley
Olive oil
Salad vinegar (Heinz is best!)
Salt & pepper

Combine beans, chopped onion, parsley and tomato and mix well. Salt and pepper the bean mixture. Pour olive oil over beans, using approximately 1/3 cup. Add salad vinegar – about 12 "shakes" and mix. Taste to determine if the salad needs additional oil, vinegar or salt & pepper.

This tastes great right away, but even better if it has an hour or so for flavors to blend. Add grilled French bread and you have a meal!

FRESH CORN AND TOMATO SALAD
SERVES 4

This is another recipe that is requested on a regular basis. Super easy. The secret? BUTTA. Make sure you use real butter not margarine. Wonderful tasty side dish to fish, chicken or beef.

> 6 ears of sweet corn – or one package frozen corn
> 4 roma tomatoes, cut into bite size pieces, seeds removed
> 1 large red onion, chopped
> 1/4 to 1/2 cup butter, cut into 4-5 pieces
> **Salt & pepper, 1 tablespoon each**
> 1 avocado, cut into bite size pieces *(optional)*

If using fresh corn, husk corn and discard husk and silk. Using a sharp knife, balance ear upright on a cutting board and cut corn off each ear.

Put cut corn and onion into a large non-stick frying pan and add butter. Heat pan to medium-high heat, stirring constantly until onion is softened, about 5 minutes. Add salt and pepper and stir to thoroughly combine. Add tomatoes and mix well. Heat through – about 3 minutes. Add avocado if using and mix well.

Remove from heat, serve and enjoy!!!!

Meat, Potatoes & a few great Mexican dishes

This section consists of meat and potatoes with a few Mexican dishes thrown in. Always good, right? You may notice I don't have as many entrée recipes as appetizers and sides. Again, that reflects the way we like to gather and entertain. Less formal. BUT, when we do have a sit down, I love nice, high quality cuts of meat simply grilled, broiled or baked as it sets the stage beautifully for potatoes. My favorite food ever. Many fantastic potato recipes here.

Now about the Mexican dishes. I wasn't sure where to put them. So here is where they landed! These are "must tries." Love them both, but especially crazy for the spinach enchiladas.

Grilled Rib Eye Steaks
Mom's Lasagna
Beef Tenderloins
Roasted Lemon Chicken
Beer Butt Chicken
Spinach Enchiladas
Chicken Enchiladas
Cheese Scalloped Potatoes
Traditional Potato Salad
Crab Stuffed Twice Baked Potatoes
Green Onion & Olive Oil Potato Salad
Loaded Smashed Potatoes
Twice Baked Potato Cups
Easy Pulled Pork
Chicken Legs
Mom's Awesome Ham Strata

BEEF TENDERLOIN STEAKS WITH MARSALA SAUCE
SERVES 8

Olive oil
4 beef tenderloin steaks, 8 ounces each
4 tablespoons butter
1 cup chopped leek *(white & pale green parts only)*
4 teaspoons minced garlic
4 cups sliced mixed fresh wild mushrooms *(any kind)*
2/3 cup dry marsala
2/3 cup beef stock or canned broth

Melt 2 tablespoons butter in heavy large skillet over medium-low heat. Add leek and garlic and sauté until almost tender, about 5 minutes. Increase heat to medium-high. Add mushrooms and sauté until golden brown, about 5 minutes. Add marsala and stock and boil until liquid is reduced by half, about 4 minutes. Strain sauce, reserving mushrooms and sauce separately.

Brush tenderloins with olive oil. Sprinkle with salt & pepper. Heat cast iron grill pan over medium-high heat until slightly smoking. Grill to desired doneness, about 4 minutes per side for medium-rare. Once done, transfer to a platter and let rest. (If cooking in the oven, cook at 375 degrees for approximately 30-35 minutes for medium rare).

Bring sauce to simmer in heavy large skillet. Remove skillet from heat. Gradually whisk in remaining 2 tablespoons butter. Add reserved mushrooms and stir over low heat until mushrooms are heated through, about 2 minutes. Season to taste with salt & pepper. Place steaks on platter. Spoon sauce and mushrooms over sirloin. Serve!

GRILLED RIB EYE STEAKS
SERVES 2

The rib eye is my favorite steak. Probably because it contains a fair amount of fat which makes it super tender and simply delicious. I serve this – and all steaks – with black or white truffle oil. Drizzle some of this on your steak and you will swoon. Another favorite – that is incredible as well – is truffle butter. Put pieces of butter on your steak. Amazing. Both truffle oil and truffle butter are getting much easier to find. Most gourmet grocery stores carry them.

Truffle oil is awesome drizzled over roasted potatoes as well.

A ribbed cast iron pan is perfect for grilling steaks indoors. If you don't have one buy one. A worthwhile investment.

2 rib eye steaks
Olive oil
Salt & pepper
2 yellow or white onions, sliced into thick rings
Truffle oil and/or truffle butter

Preheat oven to 450 degrees. Place steaks on a cookie sheet and allow to come to room temperature. Drizzle steaks with olive oil and season with generous amounts of salt and pepper.

Lightly oil a cast iron ribbed skillet and place in preheated oven. Heat 2 tablespoons olive oil in a non-stick frying pan over medium-high heat until hot and slightly smoky. Add onions and sauté, stirring occasionally, until onions are light brown. About 6-7 minutes. Remove from heat.

For medium-rare steaks, pull skillet out of the oven and place over medium-high burner. Add rib eyes and sear on each side for 2-3 minutes. Put steaks back in oven for about 5 minutes. Remove and continue to cook over burner for 2 minutes. Remove from heat, plate and add fried onions.

NOTE: Steaks are medium-rare if when you push on the thickest part of the steak it slowly springs back. Steaks are rare if steak remains indented, and well-done if it is difficult to push down and springs back immediately.

MOM'S LASAGNA
SERVES 8

My sisters and I grew up with this amazing lasagna and still swear it is the very best lasagna ever. You can substitute the same amount of ground beef for the sausage if desired – but Italian sausage is so darn good.

1-1/2 pounds Italian sausage, remove casing and cut into bite size pieces
1 garlic clove, minced
1 tablespoon parsley
1 tablespoon basil
1-1/2 teaspoon salt
2 pounds canned, diced tomatoes
2 six ounce cans tomato paste
1 package lasagna noodles, cooked
3 cups cottage cheese
2 eggs, beaten
2 tablespoons parsley
1/2 cup Parmesan cheese
12 large slices Mozzarella cheese

Preheat oven to 375 degrees. In large frying pan, brown Italian sausage and place cooked sausage on paper towels to drain. Set aside.

In a large pot combine garlic, parsley, basil, salt, canned tomatoes and tomato paste. Add Italian sausage and simmer for 1 hour, stirring occasionally.

In separate bowl, combine cottage cheese, beaten eggs, parsley and Parmesan cheese. Mix well.

Lighty grease a 9x13 inch casserole dish – I prefer glass dishes. Cover the bottom of a large casserole dish with cooked lasagna noodles, overlapping slightly. Spoon half of the cottage cheese mixture over noodles. Cover the cottage cheese mixture with slices of Mozzarella cheese. Cover the Mozzarella cheese with the tomato and meat sauce mixture.

Repeat layers. Cook in preheated oven for 40-50 minutes, until lasagna is bubbling. Cool briefly and serve.

ROASTED LEMON CHICKEN
SERVES 2

Lemon is great on so many different kinds of food – and chicken is no exception.

    1 3-4 pound whole chicken
    2 lemons, cut cross-wise into 1/4 inch slices, plus 1 lemon cut into wedges
    Garlic salt
    1/4 cup to 1/3 cup butter, softened
    Pepper
    Olive oil
    1 large white onion, cut into wedges
    3-4 small red or white potatoes, cut into wedges

Preheat oven to 350 degrees. Wash chicken thoroughly. Pat dry. With clean hands, gently pull chicken skin away from meat, starting at the neck and working your way to middle of chicken. Do the same thing starting from the "butt" and working your way to the middle of the chicken as well. Repeat the process on the drumsticks.

Rewash hands and take a chunk of softened butter in one hand, hold up one side of chicken skin and work your hand under the skin, spreading the butter onto the chicken meat. Repeat until all chicken meat is covered with a layer of butter.

Now pull skin gently up again and shove lemon slices as far under skin as possible and continue putting lemon under skin until all lemon is used and most of chicken is covered. Smooth skin down.

Rub olive oil over chicken skin and sprinkle liberally with salt and pepper. Put chicken in an oven proof skillet. Scatter cut onions and potatoes around the chicken, drizzle with olive oil and sprinkle with salt and pepper.

Put chicken in oven on the middle or lower rack and cook 15 minutes per pound, or about 45 minutes. The chicken is done if when pierced the "juice" is clear. Cut chicken into halves, place on 2 dinner plates and remove lemon from chicken. Spoon potatoes and onions onto plates. Place 2 lemon wedges on each plate, serve and enjoy!

BEER BUTT CHICKEN
SERVES 2

So love this fun, fun chicken dish. Absolutely delicious and comical to make!

This works great on the grill too!

1 whole chicken, 3-4 pounds
1 large white onion, cut into wedges
1 can beer – no bottles, use canned beer!
Pepper
Lawry's seasoned salt
Olive oil
Several small white or red potatoes

Preheat oven to 350 degrees. Put rack low in the oven. Clean chicken thoroughly. Open your CAN of beer and if you are so inclined, chug about half of it. I prefer Bud Light Lime (and except for this recipe, always in either glass bottles or the awesome resealable plastic bottles). Place can in a heavy duty pan (I use cast iron) and shove the beer can up the chicken's butt so that the chicken is sort of standing in the pan…held up by the can up its butt, of course.

Now drizzle olive oil on chicken and sprinkle to taste with pepper and seasoned salt – or anything else that turns you on. Stuff the top of the chicken with some of the onions and scatter the rest in the bottom of the pan.

Cut the potatoes into wedges and mix with the onions in the pan. Season with salt and pepper. There should be olive oil in there as well from drizzling the chicken, but add more if you don't care about the fat.

Put pan in oven and cook for about 15 minutes per pound.

When done, pull onions out of the chicken, cut up and serve with potato mixture. I usually also serve it with broiled asparagus and mushrooms (mixed up with olive oil).

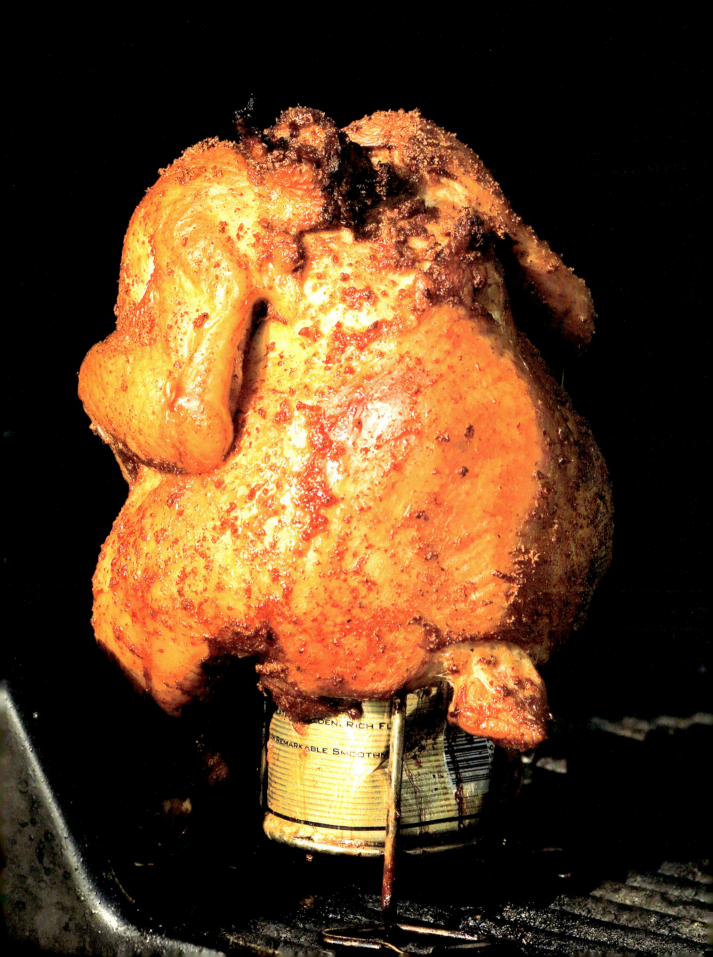

SPINACH ENCHILADAS
SERVES 4 (Makes 8)

When I lived in Knoxville, Tennessee, I had a favorite Mexican restaurant I frequented almost every weekend. La Paz had the best con queso dip – the best margarita's (rocks, no salt) and the BEST spinach enchiladas ever. I remember recreating these for a party and guests telling me they were as good as the La Paz version – how awesome is that! Try these. Even if you don't like spinach, you will love these.

3 packages frozen spinach, thawed and squeezed dry
10 large tortillas
2 cups shredded Pepper Jack cheese, plus more to top enchiladas
1 eight ounce brick light cream cheese
8 green onions, chopped
1 cup red salsa, mild or hot
1/2 cup green salsa, mild or hot
1 can green chilies, drained and chopped
Garlic salt
1 can enchilada sauce

TOPPINGS
Green or red salsa
Chopped green onion
Sour Cream
Jalapeños, chopped
Guacamole

Preheat oven to 350 degrees. Spray vegetable oil in large casserole dish and set aside. In a large bowl, combine spinach, 2 cups shredded cheese, 1 cup chopped green onion, 1 brick of cream cheese, 1/2 cup green salsa and jar of drained green chilies. Mix well, thoroughly combining ingredients. Add garlic salt to taste and mix.

Spoon 3 or more heaping tablespoons of mixture on one end of each tortilla, leaving about 1 inch bare on each side. Fold bare ends over spinach mixture (and keep each side folded down entire tortilla) and roll the tortilla into tube shape. Place tortilla, end side down, cross-wise in prepared casserole dish. Continue to fill each tortilla and place in dish. Once all tortillas are complete, pour jar of enchilada sauce on top of tortillas.

Bake in preheated oven for about 45 minutes. After 25 minutes, pull enchiladas from oven and top with additional shredded Pepper Jack cheese and 1 cup red salsa. Place back in oven for remaining 20 minutes, or until cheese is melted and enchiladas are hot throughout. Remove from oven and serve with toppings.

Meat & Potatoes 101

MARY PAT'S CHICKEN ENCHILADAS
SERVES 6

My friend Mary Pat is an avid cook and also supplies a local gourmet grocery store with her delicious tiramisu. I have also included one of Mary Pat's pasta recipes I serve when comfort food is a must.

- 1 purchased cooked rotisserie chicken
- 1 large can mild or hot enchilada sauce, divided
- 1 small can diced green chilies, do NOT drain
- 2 cups mushrooms, sliced thin and lightly sautéed in 2 tablespoons olive oil
- 3 cups Jack cheese, divided
- 1/4 cup sour cream
- 1 package medium sized flour tortillas

Preheat oven to 350 degrees. Spray the bottom of a 9x13 inch pan with non-stick cooking spray. Pour 1/2 cup enchilada sauce on bottom of pan to coat.

Mix diced chicken, green chilies, mushrooms, 2 cups cheese and sour cream in a large bowl. Fill tortillas with 1/2 cup mixture and roll up. Place snugly in pan. Continue filling until mixture runs out. Pour remaining enchilada sauce over tortillas and top with remaining cup cheese.

Bake at 350 for about 30-40 minutes, until heated through. Serve with diced avocado, sour cream and jalapeños.

EASY PULLED PORK
SERVES 6-8

Terrific summer outdoor party food. Easy to prepare – just sear, put in slow cooker and walk away for hours. Perfect!

> 5 pound pork butt
> Paprika, garlic salt and pepper
> 3-4 tablespoons vegetable oil
> 3 garlic cloves, crushed
> 2 tablespoons cracked pepper
> 2 bottles beer
> Water
>
> SPICES USED after pork butt is cooked:
> **Cider vinegar**
> **Your favorite BBQ sauce**

Generously sprinkle meat with paprika, garlic salt and pepper. Add oil to a large frying pan and heat until very hot. Once hot, sear pork butt on all sides to form a crust, about 3 minutes each side.

Place seared pork butt in a slow cooker. Add water, beer, garlic and pepper. Cover and simmer on low heat for 4-5 hours. Remove pork butt, and with 2 forks, pull pork from bone and shred meat. Add a few "shots" of cider vinegar. Taste and adjust spices accordingly adding salt, pepper, more cider vinegar if desired.

When serving, have a bottle of BBQ sauce available for guests as well.

CHICKEN LEGS
SERVES 12

These are great for outdoor BBQ's and tailgates. They look pretty and are delicious and easy to eat. NOTE: these need 4-5 hours to brine in fridge prior to cooking. This plumps the legs up and infuses them with the brine flavor. Add additional spices you like. We sometimes use soy sauce. Another great flavor.

12 large chicken legs
BBQ sauce
Garlic salt

BRINE
Half gallon water
1/2 cup salt
1/2 cup sugar
4 garlic cloves, crushed

Combine chicken legs and brine. Mix well. Put in a large pot or large Ziplocs and refrigerate for 4-6 hours. Preheat oven to 350 degrees. Remove chicken from refrigerator, discard brine and rinse chicken legs. Pat chicken dry. Put chicken on broiler pan, brush with BBQ sauce and sprinkle with garlic salt. Cook for about 25 minutes. Adjust oven temperature to low broil. Broil for just a few minutes to crisp chicken legs. Remove from oven and check doneness by cutting into "fat" part of leg. If still pink, reduce heat to 350 degrees and cook for another 5 minutes or so until no longer pink. NOTE: If you want more BBQ sauce on chicken legs, brush more on prior to broiling or heat up your sauce and apply when chicken is removed from the oven.

Serve immediately and enjoy!

MOM'S AWESOME HAM STRATA
SERVES 8

Another family favorite we count on enjoying when we all get together. Mom never lets us down! Try this and you will not be disappointed. Note: This needs to sit in the refrigerator overnight, so plan accordingly.

- 10 eggs
- 2-1/2 cups skim milk
- 2 tablespoons dijon mustard
- 1 pound ham, thinly sliced
- 1 loaf white bread, preferably unsliced from your favorite bakery
- 10 ounces Sharp Cheddar cheese, shredded
- 5 chopped green onions *(optional)*
- 2 teaspoons salt
- 1 teaspoon pepper
- Butter to grease casserole dish

Butter a 9x12 inch casserole dish. In a large bowl, beat eggs and add milk, salt, pepper and mustard. Mix well. Add onions if using. Set aside.

Cut or rip bread into 1 inch pieces. Put half of bread into the casserole dish. Top with half of the ham and half of the cheese.

Layer remaining bread and repeat toppings. Pour egg mixture on top of bread/cheese. Cover with foil and refrigerate overnight. About half an hour before cooking, preheat oven to 350 degrees. Remove strata from the refrigerator and allow to sit for 30 minutes.

Cook the strata for about an hour and 15 minutes. Check it after 1 hour. It should be puffy and light brown. Strata shouldn't be "jiggly" in the center, so cook a bit longer if needed. Cool slightly and serve. I like to serve this with fruit salad and mimosa's. I'm getting hungry…and thirsty just thinking about this!

TWICE BAKED POTATO CUPS
SERVES 8

My good friend Lisa's recipe. These little potato cups are absolutely delicious and can be served as a side dish as well as an appetizer. Make sure you get small potatoes. You can make these up to 2 days ahead – which makes it even better.

4 small russet potatoes, scrubbed
Vegetable oil
1 cup coarsely grated Havarti cheese *(about 4 ounces)*
1/2 cup sour cream
1/2 cup whole milk
1/4 teaspoon cayenne pepper
3 tablespoons butter
1-1/2 cups thinly sliced shallots, *(or onions)* **about 8 ounces**

Preheat oven to 400 degrees. Pierce potatoes in several places with fork, then brush lightly with oil. Place potatoes directly on oven rack and bake until potatoes can be pierced easily with a fork or knife, about 45-55 minutes. Cool potatoes slightly.

Lower oven temperature to 350 degrees. Cut off thin slice from both short ends of each potato. Cut each potato crosswise in half; stand each half on its small flat end. Scoop out cooked potato from each half to form upright potato cup.

Place the potato cups in a glass baking dish. Put all the scooped potato in a bowl and add cheese, sour cream, milk and cayenne. Use a potato masher or fork and mash together until it's almost smooth. Add salt and additional cayenne pepper to taste. Scoop mixture into each potato cup until full and mounded slightly.

If not serving immediately, refrigerate potato cups for up to 2 days.

Bake the cute little potato cups in preheated oven for about 20 minutes. While potato cups are cooking, melt butter in skillet over medium heat. Add shallots (or onion) and sauté until a deep brown, about 10 minutes. Top the potato cups with the shallots and serve.

LOADED SMASHED POTATOES
SERVES 6-8

This dish combines unexpected ingredients to create a truly unique and flavorful potato dish. You will love it!

- **3 pounds heirloom, small red-skinned or fingerling potatoes, washed thoroughly**
- **Wedge of good quality Gorgonzola cheese, broken into small chunks**
  (should be about 1/2 cup or a little more)
- **1 bunch arugula, washed, stemmed and ripped into bite size pieces**
- **1 cup toasted pecans, broken into large pieces**
- **1/3 to 1/2 cup olive oil**
- **Salt & pepper**

In large pot, boil potatoes with skins on until they can be pierced through with a fork. Cut potatoes into 2 or 3 inch chunks if they are large. Time will vary, based on potato size and variety, 20 minutes or so. Drain and rinse potatoes. Return potatoes to drained pot. Using a potato masher or large spoon, smash potatoes until mashed but still has some potato chunks.

Add 1/3 cup olive oil and mix/mash until incorporated. Add salt and pepper, Gorgonzola cheese, pecans, 3/4 of the arugula and mix well. Top with remainder of arugula and serve immediately.

CHEESE SCALLOPED POTATOES
SERVES 10-12

Awesome side dish – this is another dish that disappears quickly. In fact, my nephews hug me when I put it on the table. You can't ask for more than that!

- 5 pounds yukon gold potatoes, washed and sliced thin with skins on
- 16 ounces Sharp Cheddar cheese, shredded
- 16 ounce container reduced fat sour cream
- 3 cans cream of onion soup *(cream of chicken soup can be used if you can't find cream of onion)*
- **Salt & pepper**

Preheat oven to 375 degrees. Spray a 9x13 inch glass casserole dish with cooking spray. In large sauce pan over a medium-high heat, combine onion soup, Cheddar cheese and sour cream. Cook until hot and bubbly, stirring constantly. Season with salt & pepper. Reduce heat to low – stirring occassionally.

While sauce is on a low heat, layer sliced potatoes in dish, overlapping as you go. Once all potatoes are layered, pour sauce over potatoes. You may have extra sauce. If so, pull potatoes out of oven after about 45 minutes and add the additional sauce to potatoes. Season with salt and pepper.

Cook in preheated oven for an hour. After an hour, pierce fork through potatoes in several different places. If the fork slides through easily, the potatoes are finished. If not, cook longer until a fork easily penetrates potatoes.

Serve and get hugs!

TRADITIONAL POTATO SALAD
SERVES 6-8

This is my mother's recipe and is the BEST potato salad I've ever eaten. I can't eat packaged potato salad because I've been spoiled by this delicious recipe. It is simple and full of flavor. Make a lot – if you have any left over the next day, you will be excited.

5 pounds yukon gold potatoes
1 to 1-1/2 cup mayonnaise *(light if desired)*
Dijon mustard
10 hard-boiled eggs, peeled and chilled
2 bunches green onions, chopped
Green onion purple blooms, if in season *(optional)*
Salt & pepper

Wash and dry potatoes. Cut into larger bite size pieces (do NOT peel. The skin adds texture and is where the vitamins are located!). Put potatoes into a large pot and cover with water, about an inch above potatoes. Sprinkle a tablespoon of salt into the water and boil.

Check potatoes after about 7-8 minutes. If a fork pierces the potato easily, remove from heat. If not, boil a few more minutes and continue checking. Once done, drain in a colander and rinse with cold water. Set aside until room temperature.

While potatoes are boiling, mix mayonnaise and mustard – the amount of mustard used is based on preference. I use 2-3 tablespoons.

In a large bowl, combine potatoes, mayonnaise/mustard mix and greens onions. Salt and pepper to taste (use a few teaspoons of each to blend flavors). Chop 8 of the chilled eggs into bite-sized pieces. Gently mix eggs into the potato salad until well blended.

At this point, determine whether you need additional mayonnaise. If serving immediately, cut two remaining hard-boiled eggs into rounds. Arrange on top of the potato salad in a circular pattern. If you have the green onion purple blossoms, scatter several on top of the salad. They are beautiful – and edible!

NOTE: If serving later, or the next day, refrigerate without the sliced eggs on top. When close to serving, you may want to add a little extra mayonnaise as it gets "sucked" into the potatoes. Add mayonnaise and top with eggs and blossoms *(if using)* and serve. Also – I don't like celery and never add it to anything. If you like it, add it!

GREEN ONION/OLIVE OIL POTATO SALAD
SERVES 10-12

I first had this potato salad at a wonderful little place called The Lunch Box. They served lunches only and it was always busy and always delicious. This tastes great and is a nice, low-fat alternative to traditional potato salad.

5 pounds small white potatoes
1 cup *(or more)* **high quality olive oil**
6-8 chopped green onions
1/4 cup chopped chives
Heinz salad vinegar
Salt & pepper

Wash potatoes well and cut into bite size pieces. Put cut potatoes in a large pot and add water until potatoes are just covered. Bring potatoes and water to boil. Boil until a fork can pierce potatoes, approximately 10 minutes. Remove from heat and drain. Rinse boiled potatoes in cold water, then place back in pot and cover with cold water for about 30 minutes.

Once potatoes are room temperature, drain potatoes and place in a large serving bowl. Add chopped green onion and olive oil. Mix well – and carefully – until well combined. Add salt and pepper to taste and thoroughly mix. Add 10 shakes of salad vinegar and mix.

Let potatoes rest for 20 to 30 minutes. Taste again and add more vinegar if desired. If it is dry add more olive oil. Serve potato salad at room temperature – it does not need to be refrigerated.

Top with chives and enjoy!

CRAB STUFFED, TWICE BAKED POTATOES
SERVES 12

This is one of my sister Anne's "signature" dishes. She really likes the phrase "signature dish" so anything you see in this cookbook from Anne will be a "signature dish." I deviate from her signature dish by eliminating the sliced Jack cheese. I like to see the crab. If you like crab – you can't beat this "signature dish"!

These are delicious cold as well, with extra sour cream.

6 idaho potatoes
1/2 cup butter, room temperature
6 green onions, chopped
Salt & pepper
2 tablespoons olive oil
1/2 cup half & half or milk
8 ounce brick of cream cheese, room temperature
1-1/2 cup shredded Monterey Jack cheese
12 slices Monterey Jack cheese, optional
1 can high quality white meat crab

Preheat oven to 350 degrees. Scrub potatoes to remove all dirt and rub with olive oil. Sprinkle with salt. Pierce potatoes in several places with a fork.

Bake potatoes for 45 minutes, or until potatoes "give" when squeezed and fork pierces easily (use oven mitts to handle potatoes). Keep oven on as you will be baking the filled crab meat potatoes as well.

Set potatoes aside until they are cool enough to handle. Cut potatoes in half lengthwise. Scoop out inside of potato, leaving 1/4 inch potato shell.

In a bowl, mash potato with butter and cream cheese until smooth. Add milk or half & half in stages to achieve desired consistency (mixture should be smooth, but thick). Add 2 teaspoons salt and 1 teaspoon pepper and combine.

Drain can of crab meat and flake meat apart. Add crab meat and shredded cheese to potato mixture, once again mixing well.

Fill potato skins with potato/crab mixture and place on a cookie sheet. Top each potato with a slice of Monterey Jack cheese. Cook potatoes in preheated oven for about 30 minutes, or until cheese slices melt and potato is heated through.

Top cooked potatoes with chopped green onion, serve and enjoy!!

Pasta & Rice

More meal options. Pasta and rice are versatile and can be served to both vegetarians and meat lovers. Vegetables are a terrific match for pasta or rice, and meat is an easy add-on if desired. These are my personal favorites.

Spaghetti Carbonara

Tomato, Basil & Brie Pasta

Linguini with Bacon and Cheese

Lemon Pasta

Classic Spaghetti & Meatballs

Pesto Pasta with Scallops

Cavatappi with Gorgonzola & Tomatoes

Paella

Killer Mac & Cheese

Kalamata Cheese Pasta Salad

Black Bean Risotto Entrée

SPAGHETTI CARBONARA
SERVES 2

I am crazy about carbonara – and this is my go-to. I have changed, adjusted, altered and refined it many times over the past couple of years. This is the end result. I hope you like it as much as I do.

4 ounces pancetta, cut into bite size pieces
1/3 cup Pecorino Romano, packed *(extra to top pasta)*
1/3 cup Parmesan, packed *(extra to top pasta)*
2 large eggs plus 2 large egg yolks
Olive oil
12 ounces spaghetti, cooked
Salt & pepper

Fill large pot halfway with water, add 1 teaspoon salt and set aside. In a medium bowl, whisk eggs, egg yolks, both cheeses and 1/2 teaspoon salt and 1/2 teaspoon pepper.

Begin to heat water in the pot. While heating, pour a small amount of olive oil in a frying pan, heat and add pancetta. Fry a few minutes until crisp. Remove from pan, set on paper towels to drain.

Once water is boiling, add spaghetti and cook until al dente. Drain, reserving 1 cup of pasta water. Put drained noodles in the pancetta frying pan over a low heat, stir for about 2 minutes. Remove from heat and add the egg mixture and pancetta. Stir well. Add some of the reserved pasta water if you want to thin the carbonara some. Salt and pepper to taste. Transfer pasta to serving bowl and sprinkle with some reserved cheese. Voila! Enjoy…….so good.

TOMATO, BASIL AND BRIE PASTA
SERVES 6-8

This pasta dish is a real treat. I love soft cheeses. I use Brie in this, but if you prefer another type of soft cheese, feel free to swap it out.

Any soft cheese rind can be removed easily if you put the cheese in the freezer for about 40 minutes before using.

1 pound linguine pasta
6 plum tomatoes
1 cup fresh basil
Juice of 2 lemons
2 tablespoons lemon zest, finely grated
1/2 cup extra virgin olive oil
Garlic powder
Salt & pepper
1-1/2 cups chopped Brie cheese, rind removed

In a large bowl, combine olive oil, lemon, garlic powder and whisk until well blended. Cut cheese into bite size pieces and set aside. Cook pasta according to directions. While pasta is cooking, cut roma tomatoes into bite size pieces and basil into thin strips.

Drain pasta and immediately toss with olive oil mixture. Add cheese, tomatoes and basil. Toss to combine. Salt and pepper to taste. Serve immediately.

LINGUINE WITH BACON AND CHEESE
SERVES 6

Mary Pat's bacon lover's dream pasta. So very good…but what isn't good with bacon?

1 pound bacon
1 package linguine
4 large shallots, chopped
1 cup heavy cream
1/2 cup sun-dried tomatoes, sliced – or 4 fresh roma tomatoes, chopped
2 cartons mushrooms, sliced *(use your favorites)*
1/2 cup freshly grated Parmesan or Romano cheese
Salt & pepper
4 tablespoons toasted pine nuts

In large frying pan cook bacon until almost crisp. Drain bacon grease from pan, reserving 2 tablespoons. Add reserved grease along with 2 tablespoons olive oil back to pan and bring to a medium-low heat.

Add shallots and mushrooms and sauté until tender. Add cream and bring to boil. Once boiling, turn heat to low and add tomatoes and bacon. Stir occasionally while making pasta.

Cook linguine to order. Drain and return to pot. Add 1/4 cup cheese, mix well and season with salt and pepper. Add tomato and bacon mixture to pasta and stir well. Top with the extra cheese and pine nuts. Settle back and enjoy the bacon!

LEMON PASTA
SERVES 4

I am crazy for lemons. Such wonderful flavor and so good for you! This recipe includes morel mushrooms – which are fabulous – but it is an optional ingredient as morels are seasonal and can be expensive. You can add other favorite mushrooms or simply leave them out.

Remember, with all dishes, you can simply add more oil and spices should you want to change the consistency and flavor intensity.

2/3 box of angel hair pasta
1 1/3 cup finely grated Asiago cheese
1/3 to 1/2 cup olive oil
4 medium size morel mushrooms, chopped
1 large lemon or 2 small lemons
1 tablespoon sea salt
1 tablespoon black pepper

Zest lemons. Cut lemons in half and set zest and lemons aside. In large pot, boil water. Add pasta and cook until al dente, about 5 minutes. Drain pasta.

Put pasta back in large bowl and add 1/3 cup olive oil and mix well with pasta tongs. Squeeze juice of lemon into pasta then add lemon zest, salt, pepper and grated cheese (reserving 2-3 tablespoons to top pasta). Add mushrooms if using. Thoroughly combine ingredients by tossing pasta.

Put pasta in a large serving bowl. Top with reserved cheese and serve!

Pasta & Rice 125

CLASSIC SPAGHETTI & MEATBALLS
SERVES 6-8

A must-have recipe as I do not know many people who don't love spaghetti and meatballs. We grow most of the vegetables and spices in our garden, so fresh ingredients are used. Although the addition of canned tomatoes and tomato paste aid in thickness, try to use as many fresh vegetables as possible, even in the winter. The end result is worth it. If you grow tomatoes and other spices, make and freeze the sauce this summer. You will have a wonderful, fresh-tasting sauce in the dead of winter.

SAUCE
- 10 roma or 6 beefsteak tomatoes, seeded removed and chopped
- 4 teaspoons oregano
- 4 slivered fresh basil leaves
- 2 medium chopped white or yellow onions
- 1/2 cup red wine (I prefer Chianti, but any red will do)
- 2 tablespoons minced garlic
- 1 tablespoon sugar
- 2 6 ounce cans tomato paste
- 1 8 ounce can crushed tomatoes, drained
- 1 cup fresh sliced mushrooms (optional)

As always, leave out any vegetables you don't like.

Sauce can be reheated several times. Add more wine or water to thin if needed.

Preheat oven to 350 degrees. In a large pot, combine all above ingredients. Heat over medium-high heat. Stir with a wooden spoon. Cover and turn heat down to medium-low, so sauce simmers. Simmer, covered for about 1 hour, 45 minutes, stirring occasionally. When about 1 hour from serving, uncover sauce. If too thin, increase heat to medium-high (sauce should boil) for about 10-15 minutes and then lower back to simmer, uncovered. If too thick, add water and/or wine slowly until desired consistency and lower heat slightly. Continue to simmer sauce, covered.

MEATBALLS
- 1-1/2 pounds 85-15 lean ground beef
- 2/3 cup fine breadcrumbs
- 2 eggs, beaten
- 1/3 cup finely-ground Parmesan cheese
- 1/4 cup minced onion
- Salt & pepper

Combine all ingredients in a large bowl and mix with your hands until well blended. Still using hands, roll meat into 1 to 1-1/2 inch balls and place on a

CLASSIC SPAGHETTI & MEATBALLS
(continued)

nonstick cookie sheet(s). Do not allow meatballs to touch on cookie sheet or they will steam, rather than cook. If you want to add the meatballs to the sauce and not serve separately, cook meatballs in preheated oven for 15 minutes. Remove from oven. Using a slotted spoon to remove grease, transfer meatballs into simmering spaghetti sauce. Stir sauce and lower heat slightly.

If serving meatballs on top of the sauce, cook meatballs in preheated oven for 25 minutes. Remove from oven and cover to keep warm.

Prepare pasta of choice according to directions. Drain. To serve – arrange pasta on each plate. Top with sauce and finish with meatballs. Sprinkle freshly grated Parmesan cheese on top and enjoy!

PESTO PASTA WITH SCALLOPS
SERVES 4

This is an excellent first course or main dish. I use this as a first course when hosting a dinner party that is meant to be long and relaxing. Courses give you and your guests time to enjoy each small plate – and allows your stomach time to let you know when it's full. I like to use penne or curly pasta, but any type will work. NOTE: You will need a food processor to make the pesto.

3 to 4 garlic cloves *(depends on your love of garlic...more or less)*
2/3 cup pine nuts
3/4 cup good Parmesan-Reggiano cheese, grated *(plus extra for garnish)*
1 teaspoon salt
1 teaspoon pepper
3 plus cups packed fresh basil
2/3 cup extra virgin olive oil
16 large sea scallops
Half a box/container of curly pasta

To make pesto: With food processor running, add garlic cloves and finely chop. Stop and add nuts, cheese, basil, salt and pepper. Process until finely chopped. While motor is running, add olive oil and blend. Set pesto aside. Prepare pasta.

While pasta is cooking, heat a pan on stove top. Add 3 tablespoons olive oil and 2 tablespoons butter. Heat until melted and pan is slightly smoking.

Add scallops. Cook for approximately 3 minutes. Turn scallops over and cook for another minutes or two. Scallops should have a nice brown crust on each side. Cook longer if you like scallops well done. Remove from heat, cover and set aside.

Drain pasta and add enough pesto to taste. (Note: You will have a good amount of leftover pesto. It will last for about one week in the refrigerator or can be frozen). Mix until combined.

Put large scoop pesto pasta on each plate. Top each plate of pasta with 4 sea scallops. Grate cheese on top and serve.

PAELLA
SERVES 8-10

I am actually not a big fan of rice, (a few favorites in this) but do love paella. Paella is a delicious dish that is a lot of fun to make - and serve - to a group of friends. Serve with your favorite sangria and the meal is done! NOTE: A paella pan, or another very large, fairly deep pan is a must.

A paella pan—or another very large, deep pan is a must.

1 frying chicken cut into 8-10 pieces
3 chorizo sausages
5 plum tomatoes cut into wedges
1 large white onion, chopped
1/4 cup olive oil
Pinch saffron
Paprika
1 pound large shrimp
6 cups water
12-15 little neck clams
2-3 lobster tails
Garlic salt
4 cups Spanish rice
Salt & pepper *(add several times during cooking process)*

Crush saffron thread to extract the most flavor.

Season chicken pieces with paprika, garlic salt and pepper. Heat oil over medium high heat. In a large paella pan, cook chicken, skin side down, until brown. Remove and set aside.

Cut chorizo into 1 inch pieces and set aside.

Add chopped onions to pan and sauté until tender. Add chopped tomatoes, stir and sprinkle with 1 tablespoon garlic salt. Continue cooking until tomatoes are soft. Add the rice and stir to coat rice with oil. Add the water. Simmer over medium high heat until rice absorbs the water, 10-15 minutes, stirring occasionally. Turn heat down to medium and add the chicken and chorizo. Gently stir. Add a pinch of saffron.

Add the shrimp and clams, pushing them into the rice to cook. Shake the pan to coat/mix. Let everything simmer for 12-15 minutes without stirring. About 10 minutes into this, add the lobster and cook another 5 minutes or so. Bring paella pan to your table. Have several large serving spoons available and let everyone help themselves. Beautiful dish – and fun to serve.

KILLER MAC & CHEESE
SERVES 10

My husband Chris put this together for one of the many family farm parties we have. It was such a hit with kids – and parents – we continue serving as it has become a disappointment if it does not appear on the table during family get-togethers.

1 large box curly pasta
1/2 package Velveeta cheese
1 eight ounce package shredded Sharp Cheddar cheese
2 tablespoons butter
8 ounces sour cream
Half & half or milk, 1/3 to 1/2 cup

In a large pot, cook pasta according to package directions. While the pasta is cooking, prepare cheese sauce. In another large pot combine cheeses, sour cream, butter and milk. Add 1/3 cup milk initially. Heat sauce and cook over medium heat, stirring constantly until cheeses are melted and ingredients combined.

Drain cooked pasta and put back in pot. Pour hot cheese sauce over pasta and mix thoroughly. If you desire the sauce to be a bit thinner, add additional milk or half & half. Continue cooking over medium heat, stirring, for about 10 minutes.

If not serving the macaroni and cheese immediately, spoon into a crock pot and put heat on medium low. It can stay in the crock pot for a couple of hours – so super easy. Just put bowls and spoons nearby and you are done!

KALAMATA CHEESE PASTA SALAD
SERVES 8

This is a very tasty side dish that is easy to make and impressive to serve. This is an entrée if topped with beef, chicken or seafood.

I use kitchen scissors to cut pasta into 2-3" pieces so eating the pasta is more manageable.

1 package angel hair pasta
1 cup fresh Parmesan cheese, grated – or Feta cheese
1 jar pitted kalamata olives, halved
Olive oil
1 bunch green onion, chopped
Salt & pepper to taste

Cook pasta to taste (I prefer al dente). Drain and rinse with cool water.

Put pasta back in pan and add approximately 3/4- 1 cup olive oil, halved olives, 1 cup grated Parmesan cheese – or Feta, and salt & pepper.

Gently mix all ingredients until well combined. Taste pasta and add more oil, cheese, olives if desired. Pasta can be left out for several hours and served at room temperature. Otherwise refrigerate pasta until an hour before serving.

Pasta & Rice

BLACK BEAN RISOTTO ENTREE
SERVES 2

When I lived in Knoxville, Tennessee, I used to frequent a little restaurant that served a black bean and rice dish that I loved. When I moved, I re-created the dish using risotto instead of rice. Simply delicious!

1 cup risotto
Chicken broth or vegetable broth
1/2 chopped red onion
1 large can black beans, with jalapeños
1 cup shredded Sharp Cheddar cheese
1 cup salsa
Sour cream
1/2 cup chopped tomatoes
1/2 cup sliced jalapeños

Cook risotto with broth according to the instructions, adding onions while cooking. As the risotto is cooking, heat beans over medium heat until very warm, about 10 minutes.

When risotto is done, spoon onto a large platter. Top risotto with hot beans. Top beans with salsa and shredded cheese. Spoon sour cream over cheese. Finish by sprinkling jalapeños and chopped tomatoes over the sour cream. Serve with additional sour cream for those – like me – who enjoy pretty much everything in excess.

CAVATAPPI PASTA WITH GORGONZOLA & TOMATOES
SERVES 6

Delicious pasta that is easy to make and so darn good!

    3 tablespoons olive oil
    1 medium white onion, chopped
    4 garlic cloves, chopped
    1 14 ounce can diced tomatoes – or 5 fresh roma tomatoes, diced
    1/2 cup fresh basil, chopped
    1/2 cup butter, room temperature
    8 ounces Gorgonzola cheese, crumbled
    1 cup shredded fresh Romano cheese
    1 pound cavatappi pasta *(or penne if desired)*

Heat oil in large skillet, add chopped garlic and onion and sauté over medium heat for about 8 minutes or until soft. Stir in tomatoes and basil. Lower heat, cook until thickened, about 20 minutes, stirring often.

While tomato mixture is thickening, cook pasta and drain. Return pasta to pot.

Beat butter and Gorgonzola until blended. Add Gorgonzola mixture to tomatoes and whisk to combine. Once blended, add to pasta. Add Romano cheese and toss to coat. Serve immediately.

Sandwiches

I'm a huge fan of sandwiches. And they aren't just for lunch anymore. Here you will find some of my very favorites. Combine any of these with a dinner salad or cuppa soup and your meal is complete!

Tomato & Cheese Panini Sandwiches

Shrimp Rolls

French Ham & Cheese Sandwiches

Stinky Ham & Cheese Sandwiches

Flank Steak & Cheese Sandwiches

Stromboli

Fresh Mozzarella, Tomato & Basil Sandwiches

Tomato, Mozzarella & Avocado Sandwich

TOMATO & CHEESE PANINI SANDWICHES
SERVES 1

I am a huge fan of panini sandwiches – so it is best to use a panini machine for this. It's well worth the investment as they are so versatile. However, if you do not have a panini maker you can use a ridged cast iron skillet to cook the sandwich and top it with another smaller, heavy cast iron skillet. Below are my favorites, but try your own favorite ingredients for "signature" paninis – the sky is the limit!

2 slices whole wheat bread or sour dough bread
1 sliced tomato
Cheese *(I usually use fresh Mozzarella, but you can use whatever strikes you that day)*

OPTIONAL INGREDIENTS
Fresh basil
Onion
Olives
Pepperoncinis

Heat the panini maker on high. While the panini maker is heating, brush one side of each piece of bread with butter or olive oil (I prefer olive oil). When the green light indicates you're ready to go, open the machine and place one piece of bread, oiled side down, on the maker and top with tomatoes, cheese and any other ingredient you are using. Place the remaining piece of bread on top, oiled side up. Close the lid of machine down on the sandwich and press hard. Hold for about 10 seconds and then leave the lid down for approximately 3 minutes. Raise lid and check sandwich. It should have brown grill marks on it and cheese should be melted. Cook longer if you need to – remove, cut in half and eat!

Any sandwich combination can be used on the panini maker – or cast iron skillet. I love this combo, but other favorites are turkey, cheese & avocado, ham & cheese, roast beef, cheddar cheese & onion and fresh tuna & avocado.

SHRIMP ROLLS
SERVES 6

We always spend the Fourth of July in Michiana Shores at my family's lake house. Chris and I are in charge of our family holiday feast. As I'm a big fan of lobster rolls, but didn't really want to purchase enough lobster for 17 people, I decided to simply make shrimp rolls. These were absolutely delicious – and I now prefer shrimp rolls to lobster rolls – how awesome is that financially? Give these a try. You may become a shrimp roll convert like me.

2 pounds uncooked large shrimp, shelled and deveined
1/2 cup chopped cilantro or chopped dill *(which ever you prefer)*
1/2 cup chopped red onion
Approximately 1/3 cup olive oil
Juice from 3 limes and 2 tablespoons lime zest
Garlic salt & pepper
1/3 to 1/2 cup light mayonnaise
6 sub rolls *(I prefer sub rolls, but top-split rolls can be used. If using do not butter or grill)*
Approximately 4 tablespoons butter, for sub rolls

Rinse shrimp and place in large bowl. Add enough olive oil to coat shrimp and mix well. Add lime juice and lime zest. Mix well. Let shrimp mixture sit for 1 hour.

Heat a large, heavy skillet on high heat for about 3 minutes. Add shrimp in an even layer. Do not overcrowd the skillet as it will prohibit even cooking. Cook shrimp approximately 2-3 minutes and flip each shrimp to cook other side another minute. Remove from pan, add additional shrimp and repeat the process until all shrimp are cooked. DO NOT overcook. Shrimp will continue cooking when removed from heat. NOTE: Add additional olive oil directly to skillet if needed.

Cool shrimp to room temperature. In large bowl, combine cooked shrimp, chopped onion, cilantro or dill and 1/3 cup mayonnaise. Mix well. Add additional mayonnaise if desired. Salt and pepper to taste and set aside.

When ready to serve, heat a heavy pan (cast iron grill pan works best, but any pan – or grill will work) until slightly smoking. Brush both cut sides of sub rolls with melted butter and place, buttered side down, on pan. Grill for 3-5 minutes, or until rolls are toasted brown. Removed from heat, spoon shrimp mixture into toasted rolls and serve! Really good…..think I will make some for dinner tonight.

FRENCH HAM & CHEESE SANDWICHES
SERVES 10 or more in small bites

After one of my trips to Paris, I decided to re-create several versions of the absolutely delicious sandwiches available throughout the incredible City of Light. Now I can visit Paris through my taste buds whenever desired. My ham & cheese (or jambon & fromage) sandwich is better the longer it sits after assembled. Make it at least one day prior to serving. If serving at a party with a lot of other choices, this serves approximately 10. If serving for lunch, cut into 4-5 sandwiches.

1 large French baguette – or ciabatta if preferred
1 pound thinly sliced pit ham *(or ham of your choice)*
3/4 pound thinly sliced Provolone or Swiss cheese
1 stick butter, room temperature

Preheat oven to 350 degrees. Slice bread lengthwise and lay both halves, cut side up, on prep surface. Generously butter both sides of bread.

On bottom half of bread, layer ham slices. Do not have more than two layers of ham on sandwich. Place cheese slices over ham, layering the same way.

Once finished assembling, place lid on sandwich and wrap tightly with foil.

IMPORTANT – place 2 heavy cast iron skillets over entire surface of the wrapped sandwich (or any other heavy object) for at least one hour prior to baking – and up to 36 hours in the refrigerator. This melds the ingredients and intensifies the flavors – as well as improves handling the sandwich once baked.

Bake wrapped sandwich in preheated oven for approximately 45 minutes. Remove from heat and let stand for about 10-15 minutes.

Then unwrap, slice into 4-5 servings for a small lunch – OR cut into about 3 inch slices across-wise to yield 8-10 sandwiches. Sandwich can also be sliced again cross-wise to create smaller, finger-food size sandwiches for larger, cocktail parties. These are terrific at room temperature as well.

STINKY HAM & CHEESE SANDWICHES
SERVES 12

As the name indicates, these have a wonderful, ripe cheese smell as they are made with Taleggio cheese. Extremely tasty as well!

12 sandwich buns
1-1/2 pounds thinly sliced pit ham *(or your favorite cut/type of ham)*
3/4 to 1 pound Taleggio wedge cheese
1/2 cup butter, softened

Place cheese in the freezer for about half an hour so it's easier to slice. Preheat oven to low broil.

Butter each side of bun and place on cookie sheet, buttered side up, and broil until bread is lightly browned. Remove from oven and reduce heat to 375 degrees.

Place 2 slices of ham, folded on roll bottom. Remove cheese from freezer and cut into 1/3 inch thick slices. Cover ham with cheese slices.

Assemble sandwich and wrap tightly in foil. Place each sandwich in oven and bake for 20-25 minutes, until cheese is fully melted and bread is hot.

These are delicious without any condiments, but can be served with spicy mustard and horseradish mayonnaise.

FLANK STEAK & CHEESE SANDWICHES
SERVES 4

I never had this in Paris, but made this with left-over flank steak and the only cheese I had —packaged American Cheese. It is a surprisingly delicious combination of flavors. The American cheese compliments the sandwich perfectly.

Optional: Pull some of the inside bread out of the top half of the baguette to allow room for steak, onions and cheese.

1 large crusty French baguette *(whole wheat baguette if desired)*
2 medium-sized flank steaks, cooked medium-rare or to preferred wellness
4 to 6 tablespoons butter, room temperature
Caramelized onions, if desired *(see below)*
1 package pre-sliced American Cheese

Preheat oven to 375 degrees. Slice baguette in half lengthwise and place on work surface. Generously butter both sides of bread. Grill or broil bread until buttered side is lightly brown. Slice flank steak into 1/2 inch thick slices and cover bottom piece of baguette with flank steak slices. Layer flank steak with caramelized onion, if using. Top steak and onion with American cheese. Place top of baguette on sandwich and wrap tightly with foil.

IMPORTANT – place cast iron skillets or other heavy item to completely cover sandwich. Leave skillets on sandwich one hour or up to 3 hours in a refrigerator.

Bake 40-45 minutes. Remove from oven and let stand for 10-15 minutes. Unwrap, cut and serve.

CARAMELIZED ONIONS

As onions contain natural sugar, no additional sugar is required. The slow cooking process will release the natural sugars, adding in the caramelizing process. If you prefer adding sugar to caramelize, add about 1 teaspoon for every 4-5 onions.

2 medium large white or red onions, sliced cross-wise into 1/4 inch slices
Olive oil
Salt & pepper

Coat large frying pan lightly with olive oil. Heat over medium high heat until slightly smoking. Add sliced onions, mixing to coat with oil. Cook onions over medium high heat, stirring occasionally for about 15 minutes. Add olive oil as needed. Lower heat and continue cooking until most onions are translucent, but some are brown and/or dark brown in places—about 20 minutes. Remove from heat and eat 'em up!

STROMBOLI
SERVES 4

My friend Tracie shared her recipe for this wonderful stromboli. As with many of my recipes, feel free to eliminate ingredients should you prefer something different. Example, Swiss cheese instead of Provolone; turkey or roast beef instead of ham, or pepperoni, etc. This is wonderful as an appetizer or as an entrée with a salad.

1 round of pizza dough, purchased
1/2 pound Swiss cheese, thinly sliced
1/2 pound Provolone cheese, thinly sliced
1/2 pound pepperoni pieces *(optional)*
1/2 pound ham, thinly sliced
1/2 pound turkey, thinly sliced
2 tablespoons oregano
Salt & pepper
1 egg, beaten
Chunky tomato sauce for dipping *(optional)*

Preheat oven to 375 degrees. Sprinkle flour on a counter work surface and roll out dough into an approximate 12x15 inch rectangle. Dough needs to be rolled out thinly.

One by one, layer meats and cheeses on dough, overlapping slightly and leaving 1/2 inch dough exposed on each side. Sprinkle oregano, salt and pepper over ingredients.

Beginning on one 15 inch side, tightly roll dough, tucking ingredients into dough as you roll.

Once dough is rolled into an oblong shape, seal the ends by pinching these seams tightly together (some of the cheese will escape during baking, but it still tastes great!). Brush the top and sides of the Stromboli with beaten egg, place on greased cookie sheet and bake for about 30 minutes, or until Stromboli is golden brown. Remove from oven and let cool for about half an hour before cutting.

Serve with tomato sauce, if using. Enjoy!

FRESH MOZZARELLA, TOMATO & BASIL SANDWICHES
SERVES 10

These must be made at least a day ahead as it needs to be refrigerated overnight. As I have a few vegetarians in the family, I need to make sure they have something to eat. These are terrific additions to our tailgate menus and always disappear. Even non-veggies like them!

1 large crusty French baguette
2 long or 3 round packages of Buffalo Mozzarella, cut in 3/4 inch slices
1 jar of basil pesto
5-7 roma tomatoes *(depending on size)*, **sliced in 1/2 inch slices**
10-12 fresh basil leaves

Slice bread in half length-wise. Place bread, sliced side up on work surface. Pull some of the bread out of the top portion of the baguette and discard. Removing this excess bread will allow both the mozzarella and tomatoes to lay inside the sandwich comfortably. OPTIONAL: Grill or toast bread in broiler until lightly brown. Let cool.

Spread each half lightly with basil pesto. On bread bottom, layer mozzarella slices evenly across bread. Place tomato slices on top of mozzarella and place basil leaves on top of tomatoes. Cover with the baguette top. Wrap sandwich tightly in foil.

IMPORTANT – put sandwich in refrigerator and place heavy cast iron skillets (or other heavy items) over entire surface of wrapped sandwich. Leave in refrigerator overnight and up to 36 hours. This melds ingredients and intensifies flavors – as well as improves the handling of the sandwich to cut, serve and consume.

TOMATO, MOZZARELLA & AVOCADO
SERVES 8-10

Another version of the tomato/mozzarella sandwich. I love avocado and it's a nice change from the basil version.

      1 French baguette, cut lengthwise
      2 long or 3 round packages of Buffalo Mozzarella, cut in 3/4 inch slices
      2-3 avocados, peeled and cut into 1/2 inch slices
      3-4 roma tomatoes, cut into 1/2 inch slices

Slice bread in half lengthwise. Put bread in oven on low broil, cut side up. Broil until lightly browned. Should be just 3 or so minutes, depending on your oven. On bottom piece of bread, lay avocado slices (NOTE: You can mash avocado up in a bowl, season if desired and spread mixture on bread). Next layer Buffalo Mozzarella on top of avocado. Finish with tomatoes. Assemble sandwich, press down and wrap with aluminum foil. Refrigerate overnight, weighted down with cast iron pans or other heavy items. Remove from fridge about 45 minutes before serving.
Slice and enjoy!

NOTE: Avocado can be added prior to serving if you don't toast the bread first.

Sweets

I'm not a big sweet-tooth gal, but I do occasionally like to indulge. So this section is worth blowing a bunch of calories. Have some fun and splurge!

Salty Chocolate French Bread Crackers

Blueberry Crostata

Chocolate Chip Cookies with Sea Salt

Cheesecake

Crumb Cake

Lemon Bars

Cinnamon Torte

Sugar's Toffee

Tiramisu

SALTY CHOCOLATE FRENCH BREAD CRACKERS
SERVES 10-12

This is super easy and very good. You can use whatever kind of chocolate you like best. I like to serve this on a platter with sliced pears, apples, a wedge of St. Andre cheese – and a glass of Sauterne. It is a wonderfully light and tasty end to a memorable meal.

30-36 crusty French bread crostinis
6 -7 chocolate bars *(I use Hershey bars)*
High Quality Sea Salt

Preheat oven to 450 degrees. Place bread crackers on cookie sheets. Put a piece of chocolate, sized to cracker, on each cracker. Lightly sprinkle sea salt on each piece of chocolate.

Cook until chocolate is completely melted – about 5-7 minutes. Remove from oven and cool slightly. Then lightly sprinkle each cracker again with sea salt. Serve warm or at room temperature with sliced fruit and cheese.

Leftovers are always consumed.

BLUEBERRY CROSTATA
SERVES 6

I love this dessert – it is beautiful, simple to assemble and delicious. A terrific way to highlight summer fruits.

The kids go blueberry picking every summer in Michigan. This is a great way to highlight their bounty!

DOUGH
1-3/4 cup all purpose flour
1 cup cold butter, cut into 1/2 inch cubes
1 tablespoon sugar
1/3 cup ice cold water

FILLING
3 cups blueberries
1/2 cup sugar
1 tablespoon cornstarch
Zest and juice of one lemon
2 tablespoons butter, cut into pieces
1 egg beaten
2 tablespoons sugar

Preheat oven to 350 degrees. Put a sheet of parchment paper on a cookie sheet/baking sheet and set aside. Place flour and butter and sugar in a food processor and pulse just to combine. Slowly add water while pulsing. Dough will form a ball. Remove from the processor and wrap in plastic. Put dough in the refrigerator for at least half an hour or as long as 4 days.

In a bowl combine sugar, cornstarch, lemon and lemon zest. Pour over blueberries and mix well to thoroughly combine.

When dough is chilled, sprinkle flour on a clean surface. Place dough on floured surface and let it sit for 30 to 40 minutes. After resting, roll the dough with a rolling pin into a 13 to 14 inch round. Transfer the dough round to the parchment covered sheet.

Spoon the blueberry filling onto the dough leaving 2 inches of dough uncovered. Fold the dough over the blueberries, pleating to form a flat cover leaving the center blueberries exposed.

Brush the dough with the beaten egg and sprinkle with 2 tablespoons sugar. Put on center rack and bake for 45 to 50 minutes (or a bit longer) until crust is golden brown. Let cool and serve with vanilla bean ice cream and enjoy. So good!

CHOCOLATE CHIP COOKIES WITH SEA SALT
MAKES 3 DOZEN

These are the very best chocolate chip cookies I've ever tasted. Using cake flour makes a big difference, so be sure to follow the ingredients. **NOTE: Dough needs to be refrigerated for 24 hours and up to 72 hours.**

2 cups cake flour, minus 2 tablespoons
1 cup bread flour
1-1/4 teaspoon baking soda
1-1/2 teaspoon baking powder
1-1/2 teaspoon salt
1-1/4 cup butter, at room temperature
1-1/4 light brown sugar
1 cup plus 2 tablespoons sugar
2 eggs
2 teaspoons vanilla
1-1/4 pounds chocolate chips *(or discs)* **with 60% or more cacao content**
Sea Salt *(high quality)*

Cream butter and sugars together with electric mixer until light – about 5 minutes. Add eggs and mix well. Stir in vanilla.

Reduce speed to low and add dry ingredients and mix until combined – then STOP. Add chips/discs and mix gently until combined.

Wrap dough in plastic and refrigerate 24-72 hours. When ready to bake, preheat oven to 350 degrees. Take dough out of refrigerator for about an hour before baking cookies.

Line cookie sheets with parchment paper. Place 1 to 1-1/2 inch dough balls on parchment paper and flatten slightly with hand or spatula. Sprinkle high quality sea salt on top of each cookie.

Bake until golden brown, about 18-20 minutes. Cool about 15 minutes and place on wire rack to cool completely. ENJOY!

CHEESECAKE
SERVES 8

This can also be a blueberry cheesecake – have 3 cups blueberries ready to use. I always use an 8 inch springform pan because the cheesecake rises dramatically high, which I love (apparently since my fabulous daughter moved out, I'm kinda missing drama), it's cracked and brown and beautiful. If you don't really love cheesecake (I don't really love it), you will most likely love this. It doesn't taste like traditional cheesecake – it's a bit more dense and a tad less sweet. It tastes so much better.

1 package Lorna Doone shortbread cookies, crushed
   (or any other shortbread cookies)
7 tablespoons butter, melted
5 packages cream cheese, room temperature *(8 ounce packages)*
2 cups granulated or bakers sugar *(finely ground)*
5 eggs
3 cups berries, if using

Preheat oven to 350 degrees. Use an 8 inch springform pan and lightly butter. Crush cookies with the tines of a fork until crumbled. Press inside the pan. Pour melted butter over the crushed cookies and mix to incorporate. Press down with a spoon. Refrigerate until ready to use.

In a large bowl, beat cream cheese until smooth and creamy with a beater or an electric mixer. Reduce speed and add sugar. Beat 2-3 minutes. Add eggs one at a time and beat 'til smooth and creamy. Pour filling into cookie pan. NOTE: You may end up with a little too much filling. Just fill to slightly below the rim. If extra, save and make a mini cheesecake! If using blueberries, scatter 1 cup of berries on top.

Bake on center rack until filling is set – about 1 hour and 45 minutes. Check regularly. It could take longer depending on your oven. It should look split and somewhat brown on top. A knife inserted into the center of the cheesecake should come out clean or fairly clean. Center should not jiggle. Once done, cool for an hour or two.

When serving, detach from springform pan and – if using, spread remaining berries on top and around platter. Lightly push them into the top of the cake.

CRUMB CAKE
SERVES 10-12

My sister Kate gave me this recipe. This crumb cake is delicious. Part of the reason is the crumb topping is super thick, so don't think you made too much – use it all! The cake and topping together are an irresistible combination.

TOPPING
1 cup dark brown sugar
1/2 cup sugar
1-1/2 tablespoon cinnamon
1/2 teaspoon salt
1 cup butter, melted and warm
2 -1/2 cups all purpose flour
Confectioners sugar, for topping baked cake

CAKE
2-1/2 cups all purpose flour
1 teaspoon baking soda
1/2 teaspoon salt
3/4 cup unsalted butter
1-1/2 cups sugar
2 eggs
1-1/2 cups sour cream
1 teaspoon vanilla extract

Preheat oven to 350 degrees. Butter a 13x9x2 inch glass baking dish. Mix all topping ingredients (but flour and confectioners suger) until incorporated. Add flour and toss with fork until clumps form. Mixture will look slightly wet. Set aside.

In a separate bowl mix flour, baking soda, salt and set aside. Use mixer and beat butter until smooth and creamy. Add sugar and beat until fluffy. Add eggs one at a time and beat. Add sour cream and vanilla. Mix well.

Add flour mixture in 3 additions and stir or beat until incorporated and smooth. Transfer batter to baking dish. Topping – take topping mixture and with hands squeeze pieces to form small clumps. Drop clumps evenly over cake and lightly press clumps into batter. It will seem like a lot of topping – but that's a good thing.

Bake cake in preheated oven for approximately 1 hour. Topping should be golden brown on top and center will come out clean after piercing with a knife. Cool at least half an hour. Sprinkle with confectioners sugar before serving.

LEMON BARS
SERVES 8

As I have stated many times in this cookbook, I LOVE lemons! So of course I love lemon bars. A perfect end to just about any meal. Light, tart and sweet, these are delicious on their own, but even better served with a nice dessert wine.

CRUST
2 cups all purpose flour
1/2 cup sugar
1 cup butter

FILLING
4 eggs
2 cups sugar
1/3 cup fresh squeezed lemon juice
1/4 cup all purpose flour
3/4 teaspoon baking powder
Powdered sugar *(optional)*

Preheat oven to 350 degrees. Mix crust ingredients together until they form a loose dough. Press into a 9x12 inch pan until it forms an even layer. Bake for about 25 minutes until lightly browned. Set aside. Beat eggs and sugar together. Add lemon juice and mix well. Add dry ingredients and mix well. Pour over crust and bake for 25-30 minutes until set. Remove from oven and cool. Sprinkle with powdered sugar if desired. Cool completely and cut into squares. I love these!

CINNAMON TORTE
SERVES 8

This is my good friend Lisa's Aunt Maria's recipe. Lisa's mom and her 6 sisters are from Belarus. After years of forced relocation, some ended up here in the U.S. and some in Canada. These women are the definition of resilient. They love life and cherish family. It is a continuous party when they are around. It's possible they coined the term "Eat, Drink and be Merry!" So gather your family, eat this delicious torte and have some fun!

The cinnamon torte can be done a day ahead of time, that way the layers sort of gel together.

CAKE LAYERS
2-3/4 cups all purpose flour
2 tablespoons cinnamon
1-1/2 cups butter
2 cups sugar
2 eggs

Preheat oven to 375 degrees. Mix ingredients together and rest the dough for 15 minutes.

Using the bottom of a pie plate as your guide, with a pencil draw the circumference onto a piece of parchment paper. Cut out 5 circles. Gently spread 1/5 of the dough onto each parchment paper circle. It should be fairly thin. Bake each of these five torte layers on a cookie sheet, one at a time, for 12 minutes (bake until a little brown, so watch carefully because they are thin and can burn easily). Once baked let the layers cool. Peel wax paper off and store the tortes in the refrigerator until ready to fill with cream layers.

CREAM FILLING
1 liter of real cream *(2 pints)*
2 tablespoons of confectioners sugar
1 teaspoon of vanilla extract
1/4 cup chocolate shavings *(garnish)*

In a large bowl, beat cream, confectioners sugar and vanilla together with a mixer until thick and fluffy. 3-5 minutes. Refrigerate for one hour and mix briefly before using.

Lay one torte round on a serving platter and cover with 1/5 of cream filling. Top with another torte round and cover with 1/5 of cream filling. Repeat process until all torte rounds are used and spread remaining cream filling on top of torte. Sprinkle chocolate shavings on top of torte and enjoy!

SUGAR'S TOFFEE
SERVES 12

My friend Sugar gave me this recipe. By far the best chocolate toffee I've had the pleasure of enjoying.

> 1 cup sugar
> 1 cup butter
> 3 tablespoons water
> 1 teaspoon vanilla
> 1 cup crushed almonds
> 4-6 chocolate bars *(I use Hershey's)*

Spread 1/2 cup crushed almonds on a cookie sheet and set aside. In heavy saucepan, heat first 4 ingredients over medium-high heat – stirring constantly – until bubbly. This should be cooked for about 8-10 minutes, until the color is a dark caramelized color and it is smoking a bit. DO NOT under-cook as it will not harden, but don't overcook or sugar mixture will burn. The color of the toffee and the smoke are key indicators this is ready.

Pour caramelized mixture onto the crushed almonds on the cookie sheet. Let caramel cool for a few minutes.

Place unwrapped chocolate bars on hot caramelized spread and as chocolate melts spread to completely cover toffee. Once finished, spread remaining crushed almonds evenly over chocolate.

Cool toffee completely. Break into desired size toffee pieces and enjoy! SOOO good – thank you Sugar!

TIRAMISU
SERVES 10

There are many different versions and recipes of this classic Italian dessert. This is my favorite, slightly altered from the traditional version. It is terrific to serve at large gatherings for several reasons – it is fairly easy to prepare, impressive, made ahead of time and requires no cooking! Note: This can be made in one large bowl, however, it is impressive to make this in individual, clear glass cups.(You will need 10 glass cups).

25 shortbread cookies, crushed
1/4 cup amaretto
1/4 cup brandy
1/2 cup coffee liquor
1/2 cup espresso – or very strong coffee
1 pound Mascarpone cheese
6 eggs, separated
1/4 cup sugar
1/4 cup grated dark chocolate or a handful of dark chocolate covered coffee beans

In a large bowl, combine crushed cookies and amaretto and mix well. Press 1/4 of this mixture into the bottom of the 10 glass cups.

Mix the brandy, coffee liquor and espresso in a bowl. Pour 1/4 of this mixture over the cookie crust in the 10 cups. In a large bowl, combine Mascarpone cheese, egg yolks and sugar. Beat until smooth.

In another bowl, whisk or beat egg whites with an electric mixer until they are stiff, and form peaks. Fold this into the Mascarpone cheese mixture and gently continue folding until combined.

Spoon 1/4 of this onto the cookie crust. Repeat these layers until you have 4 layers total. Refrigerate overnight. Before serving, top with grated chocolate or coffee beans – or both! This can be served at room temp, so take them out of the fridge about 45 minutes prior to serving. Enjoy!

SUSAN RITTS, *Author and Owner of Putting on the Ritts Catering*

Susan has always had a big interest in food – and cooking. At a young age, Susan was the designated daughter that would fry the bacon and toast the English muffins for family Sunday brunches, make the shortbread pudding cake for birthdays and try new food combinations to spring on her parents and sisters.

After college graduation, Susan worked in media sales and started her first catering company called Salads, Etc., offering a lunch delivery service.

Eventually the "foodie" bug hit hard enough that Susan left the media world entirely and opened Putting on the Ritts. She relocated to a beautiful farm outside of Minneapolis, Minnesota, where she caters custom events and markets her Crazy Good Dressing.

ACKNOWLEDGMENTS

Many thanks...

This cookbook has been a dream of mine for many years. First and foremost, while encouraged by many, *Cooking & Entertaining with Ease* would not have come to fruition without the hard, hard work of my book designer and editor, Marci Franzen. Marci's creativity and talent – along with a true love of my recipes lit the fire under me to finally "get it done." Thank you Marci! Looking forward to volume 2.

My primary photographer, Laura was a rare find. Her mother and I met at a farmer's market. The cookbook came up in conversation and she quickly let me know her daughter was a fledgling photographer and I quickly scooped her up. Laura worked tirelessly staging, adjusting, perfecting lighting for both garden and food shots – and then trying the dishes she photographed, giving me "fresh" reactions to each dish. Laura is crazy talented. I suspect I may have to arrange my future cookbooks around her very busy schedule.

To my big, loud, crazy-fun, fantastic family. So many of these recipes never would have been created without a slightly "food-obsessed" group who love any reason to get together and celebrate. Anything!

To my gorgeous daughter Molly. She is an amazing young woman and the light of my life. As she became a vegetarian back in high school, she pushed me to broaden my food "horizons" and embrace meatless meals. Thank you.

And, of course, my husband Chris. Chris's never-ending support, crazy sense of humor, endless encouragement as well as endless culinary adventures pushed me on each time I needed pushing. And there were many of these times. Thank you honey…love you!